William Fletcher, John Reid

Truth no enemy to peace

Animadversions on the Rev. Mr. Fletcher's defence of his Scripture-Loyalist

William Fletcher, John Reid

Truth no enemy to peace
Animadversions on the Rev. Mr. Fletcher's defence of his Scripture-Loyalist

ISBN/EAN: 9783337224592

Printed in Europe, USA, Canada, Australia, Japan

Cover: Foto ©Andreas Hilbeck / pixelio.de

More available books at **www.hansebooks.com**

TRUTH NO ENEMY TO PEACE.

ANIMADVERSIONS

ON

THE REV. MR. FLETCHER's

DEFENCE

OF HIS

SCRIPTURE-LOYALIST.

SOME GENERAL PRINCIPLES STATED, AND SHORTLY ILLUSTRATED.
THE STATE OF THE QUESTION, BETWEEN SECEDERS AND DISSENTERS,
ON THE HEAD OF MAGISTRACY, ASCERTAINED, FROM THEIR
RESPECTIVE WRITINGS.

THE ARGUMENT DIVESTED OF SUCH THINGS, AS ARE, EVIDENTLY,
FOREIGN TO THE SUBJECT.

DISSENTING-PRINCIPLES SHEWN TO BE CONSISTENT WITH
THE SAFETY AND HAPPINESS OF HUMAN SOCIETY.

AND THE BIBLE FOUND TO BE THE STANDARD OF OUR CONDUCT,
IN EVERY STATION OF LIFE, WHETHER CIVIL, OR RELIGIOUS.

By *JOHN REID*,
MINISTER OF THE GOSPEL IN LAWRIESTON.

Love the truth and peace. ZECH. viii. 19.

*Be ready always to give an answer to every man, that asketh you a reason
of the hope that is in you, with meekness and fear.* 1 PET. iii. 15.

FALKIRK:
PRINTED BY T. JOHNSTON.
1799.

PREFACE.

THE Author of thefe Animadverfions is fully fenfible, that the fubject, on which he hath ventured to offer his thoughts to the public, is, at this time, exceedingly unpopular. The prevailing opinions, and common prejudices of the age, are evidently againft him. Some few, it is hoped, may ftill be found, who will allow him an attentive, and candid perufal. From thefe he expects every reafonable indulgence; trufting, that general affertions will not be over-ftrained, nor forced conclufions drawn from them; and that doubtful words, or detached expreffions will not be too feverely handled, without carefully comparing one place with another, and attending to the general fcope.

IT was not without confiderable reluctance, that he took the pen, in this controverfy. The reluctance, however, did not arife from any conviction of a bad caufe, or perfuafion of its being indefenfible. He is aware, there are many, who reckon it almoft impoffible to believe, that Diffenting Minifters can be fincere in their profeffion; hence they, very uncharitably, charge them, with wilfully leading their people aftray. But for himfelf, he can honeftly declare, and, fo far as he knows, the fame is the cafe with all his Brethren, that the longer he revolves the fubject, from year to year, in his own mind, the more clofely he attends unto it; the more deeply convinced he is, that the declarative glory of God, and the happinefs of mankind, are concerned in the caufe, for which he pleads. The perfonal infirmities of its profeffors are abundantly numerous, and mournfully great; yet the caufe itfelf feems plainly to have the fanction of a "Thus faith the Lord." Did he not, ferioufly and candidly, think fo; he never fhould wifh to defend it. But the Author's reluctance arofe from the confideration, of having little or no profpect, of making matters any better, or of bringing the difpute to a comfortable iffue. Naturally averfe to litigation, and feeing no

pro-

propriety in arguing for arguing's fake; he felt difpofed, after what hath already been advanced, on both fides of the queftion, rather to let the controverfy fleep, and leave the candid public, from henceforth, to judge for themfelves. But various concurring circumftances have led him, ftep by ftep, into the undertaking. Befides other things, which need not be mentioned, the gratifying of fellow-profeffors, who ftill wifhed to fee fomething farther, in reply to Mr. Fletcher's Defence; refpeft for the memory of our deceafed Brother, who is no more to anfwer for himfelf; and the vindication of, what appeared to him to be, one, though only one, of the important articles, in that facred depofitum, long entrufted with the Reformed Church of Scotland, at length prevailed with him, to fubmit a few thoughts to the public.

Some will, probably, be furprifed to find, that Diffenters write fo much on Magiftracy, and fo little on other fubjefts. It is not, furely, becaufe they find more pleafure in treating that, than in treating other fubjefts, or reckon it of fuperior importance to other things; but the obvious reafon is, becaufe the head of Magiftracy is that, on which they have been moft frequently, and violently, attacked, efpecially fince the commencement of the Seceffion: the law of felf-defence, therefore hath obliged them to be often in the field.

As to the prefent ftate of the difpute; if the reader wifh to have the fubjeft properly before him; it will be requifite to read, firft the particular Seftion of the Defence, animadverted upon; and then, the Animadverfions on that Seftion; together with the authorities quoted, at the bottom of the page. Having read, with candour, and impartiality, and having carefully compared the whole with the unerring ftandard; let him decide, as he may find caufe.

Lawrieston, 16*th*. March, 1799.

INTRODUCTION,

Containing a few General Principles; which, it is hoped, may be of fervice, towards the right ftating, and the terminating of the Controverfy.

EVERY perfon, of difcernment, will readily perceive, that no difpute can be managed, with propriety, unlefs we have fome firft principles, on which we all along proceed; fome things freely granted, on both fides, and always confidered as needing no further proof. Were this duly attended to, fuch principles properly afcertained, and the terms, ufed in the ftating of queftions, carefully explained, before we proceed; it is prefumed that, at leaft, the one half of the difputes, amongft Chriftians, might foon be at an end. But while there is no fixed principle, fteadily adhered unto, and while terms are freely ufed, now in one fenfe, and then in another, without ever apprizing the reader; it is fimply impoffible to decide the controverfy.

HAVING thefe views, it is hoped, the reader will be pleafed to attend unto the few following propofitions; which, being once confirmed, and held as eftablifhed maxims; the controverfy, between Seceders and Diffenters, may be the more eafily terminated. Their fubferviency to this purpofe will afterwards appear.

PRO-

PROPOSITION I.

THE Holy Scriptures, wherever they are enjoyed, fhould be confidered, and applied, as a complete rule of faith and practice, to all defcriptions of men, in every department of human life.

Owing to the depravity of our nature, by the fall, " The way of man is not in himfelf: it is not in man that walketh to direct his fteps." * The dictates of his natural judgment and confcience, unaffifted by the heavenly Oracles, are altogether infufficient to guide his feet in the path of duty; either in one ftation, or another.

In compaffion to this mournful condition, the Lord, our Lawgiver, hath favoured us with a very full, and clear revelation of his will, in the Holy Scriptures. This Revelation, evidently, contains neceffary, and fuitable directions for human conduct, in every ftation and capacity, from the king on the throne, to the meaneft beggar in the cottage.

It is indifputable, that kings, and other civil magiftrates, of old, were pofitively required, to have a copy of the divine law continually by them, to read in it, all the days of their life, and to rule their people, according to it. † The Scripture regulation ever was, " He that ruleth over men muft be juft, ruling in the fear of God." ‡ When the fweet palmift of Ifrael praved, " Order my fteps in thy word," ∤ he certainly wifhed it might be the cafe, in his public official capacity, as well as in more private ftation. Concerning the minifters of religion, this is the honourable character, " They have obferved thy word, and kept thy covenant. They fhall teach Jacob thy judgments, and Ifrael thy law." ₎ And to perfons of every defcription, in both the higher, and lower circles of life, the language of infpiration is, " To the law and to the teftimony;

* Jer. x. 23.   † Deut. xvii. 18,—20.   Jofh. i. 8.
‡ 2 Sam. xxiii. 3.   ∤ Pfal. cxix. 133.   ₎ Deut. xxxiii. 9, 10.

mony; if they fpeak not according to this word, it is becaufe there is no light in them." * Thefe laws refpect not outward wafhings, purifications, facrifices, feaft-days, or other ceremonial obfervances, emphatically ftyled, *carnal ordinances*, impofed upon the church, until the times of reformation only : no, furely ; they refpect the mental endowments, moral character, and righteous conduct of men, towards God, and towards one-another.

To convince us that, in their true fpirit and fcope, thefe are ftanding moral precepts, ftill in force, the New Teftament-Scripture tea hes, fubftantially, the fame things. There too, the n ceffary qualifications, and official duties of civil magiftrates, as well as thofe of gofpel minifters, are clearly unfolded ; while the duties of hufband and wife. parent and child, mafter and fervant, and of equals one to another, are alfo defcribed, in words which the fame Divine Spirit, who actuated the prophets of old, teacheth. † The general, and infallible affertion, concerning the Holy Scripture, is, that " It is all given by infpiration of God, and is profitable for doctrine, for reproof, for correction, for inftruction in righteoufnefs; that the man of God may be perfect, thoroughly furnifhed unto all good works." ‡ The latitude of expreffion here deferves our fpecial notice, " unto all good works." Whatever good deed he may be called to perform, and in whatever capacity he may be required to act ftill let him confider the infpired Oracles, as the great fource of his information. and the rule, which God hath given for his direction, Befides, it is exprefsly declared, that " As many as have finned in the law fhall be judged by the law." ‡

PRO-

---

* Ifa. viii. 20.   † Rom. xiii. 1. 3. 4.   Eph. vi.   Col. iii. &c.

‡ 2 Tim. iii. 16, 17.   ‡ Rom. ii. 12.

THINGS are right, or wrong, in their own nature, and as determined by the divine law; independent of the will of any man, or clafs of men, however numerous.

It is granted, that there are actions, fuch as the taking away of a man's life, on which, while barely confidered as things done, we cannot well pronounce, whether they be right, or wrong, till once they be clothed with their various circumftances. But after taking into the account the ftation and character of the agent, the fprings of action, the manner of proceeding, the law tranfgreffed, or obeyed, together with the tendency, and native confequences of the deed, and bringing the whole to the unerring ftandard; then they muft be confidered as right or wrong, according as they agree, or difagree with that ftandard: though fome fhould approve, and others condemn, and on whatever fide the majority fhould be found. It is felf-evident, that the will, or choice, of the creature can never make that ftraight, which God hath made crooked, nor the contrary.

Concerning this, the language of Scripture is plain and unequivocal. Hence we are told, " There is a way which feemeth right unto a man; but the end thereof are the ways of death." * We read of fome who " call evil good, and good evil; who put darknefs for light, and light for darknefs; who put bitter for fweet, and fweet for bitter. Who are wife in their own eyes, and prudent in their own fight." And yet they are charged with " cafting away the law of the Lord of Hofts, and defpifing the word of the Holy One of Ifrael." † Saul of Tarfus thought that he was doing God good fervice, when he was perfecuting the faints; and might have found thoufands, and ten thoufands to concur with him, in that opinion. Yea, in much later times, the great majority of many nations, at once, have

* Prov. xiv. 12. † Ifa. v. 20, 21. 24.

have, with apparent fincerity, held fuch doctrine; and their confcience feems to have approved. *

Amidft a great variety of fubordinate ftandards, it is neceffary, that there fhould always be fome general, and unerring ftandard; to which the reft may be brought, and by which they may be adjufted. The natural dictates of right reafon, as they are called, in the confciences of men, the decrees of councils, the ufages of nations, the deeds of bodies politic, and fuch like, can never be viewed in any other light, then as fubordinate fallible rules. They are often at variance amongft themfelves; and therefore can never, by themfelves, be a fufficient rule for human conduct, neither in one ftation, nor another. Hence it is plain, that, in order to afertain whether things be right, or wrong, it is not enough that we find them to be fanctioned by a majority; but we muft carefully confider their nature and tendency, and bring them, ultimately, to the unalterable ftandard of righteoufnefs.

PROPOSITION III.

As they, to whom much is given, will have more required of them, than will be of thofe, who never had any fuch light, nor means of knowledge; there can be no conclufive reafoning, from the one cafe, to the other.

Pofitively fpeaking, indeed, "Every fin, being againft the fovereignty, goodnefs, and holinefs of God, and againft his righteous law, deferveth his wrath and curfe, both in this life, and that which is to come;" it cannot, however, be refufed, that the fame evils are, comparativly, lefs, and much more excufable, in the cafe of a people who never knew any better, than they are in the cafe of fuch as have been remarkably enlightened, openly profeffed the truth, and folemnly fworn adherance unto it. This is fo exceedingly plain, from our Saviour's own doctrine, that none, who believe him to
be

* When Popery was at its height.

be the true and faithful Witnefs, can poffibly deny it.
"Unto whomfoever much is given," fays he, "of him
fhall be much required; and to whom m⸳⸳n have committed much, of him they will afk the more." * And
again, "If I had not come,and fpoken unto them they
had not had fin; but now they have no cloak for their
fin." † Their fin had been, comparatively, much lefs;
but now, having enjoyed the beft means of information,
by the clear fhining of the true light, they are altogether inexcufable ; their fin is much more aggravated;
they have much more to account for. The forecited
paffage, in the Epiftle to the Romans, teaches the fame
doctrine, "As many as have finned without the law
fhall alfo perifh without law ; and as many as have
finned in the law fhall be judged by the law." ‡ Su-
perior light fhall occafion an anfwerable account to be
given.

Following the dictates of their own confcience, and
guided by the dim taper of nature's light, even the Heathen, who are without the Scripture-Law, may do many
things materially good, and fubftantially the fame with
thofe things which are required of Chriftians. But the
queftion is not, what is, or may be done, by them; but
what is expected of us, who are favoured with the clear
fun-fhine of Divine Revelation, to guide our feet in the
way of righteoufnefs ?

˙PROPOSITION IV.

Human fociety, in general, is, or at leaft ought to be,
formed by mutual confent, either tacitly or exprefly
given ; and not by compulfion, or one party lording it
over the confcience of another.

Society hath been very juftly defined, "A number
of rational and moral beings, united for their common
prefervation and happinefs." ⊥ Is man indeed a rational
being; then his will or choice fhould certainly be influenced,

---

* Luke xii. 48   † John xv. 22.   ‡ Rom. ii. 12.

⊥ Encycl, Brit. New Edit, on Society.

fluenced, not by force, but by the dictates of a well informed underſtanding; while his underſtanding ſhould
receive its information from the revealed will of God;
" The entrance of whoſe words giveth light; and giveth
underſtanding unto the ſimple." *   If this be refuſed, it
muſt be done at the expence of degrading man from his
high rank, in the ſcale of exiſtence, and claſſing him
with the gregarious beaſts of the field; which come
together, by natural inſtinct, or the compulſory meaſures
of their rigorous lords.   Hence, the authors of the above
definition very properly obſerve, " There are ſhoals of
fiſhes, herds of quadrupeds, and flocks of birds.   We call
crows and beavers, and ſeveral other ſpecies of animals,
gregarious; but it is hardly good Engliſh to ſay that
they are *ſocial*." †   Nor would it, ſurely, be much better Engliſh to ſay, that a reaſonable, moral, and free
agent ſhould be forcibly obliged to enter into ſociety, upon conditions, which his judgment can by no means approve, after all the pains which he can take, to receive
the beſt information.

None, it is hoped, will deny, that, ſtrictly and properly ſpeaking, JEHOVAH alone is Lord of the conſcience.
It is his ſole prerogative to ſearch the heart, and try the
reins.   If ſo, whoſoever takes it upon him, to force
another into meaſures, which he cannot poſſibly approve,
undoubtedly uſurps the prerogative of the Moſt High.
There is no inconſiſtency in uſing Scriptural arguments,
and rational means, to remove his objections, and reaſon
him into compliance; but to compel he hath no power.

The Scripture ſeems plainly to teach the ſame doctrine, while it ſays, " Can two walk together except
they be agreed?" ‡   Interrogations of this kind, it is
well known, imply the ſtrongeſt negative; as much as
to ſay, it is quite inconſiſtent, it is altogether unreaſon-
able, ever to expect, that two perſons, at variance between themſelves, ſhould have the benefit, and the
comfort of ſocial intercourſe by the way; or, that they
ſhould heartily combine their counſels, and unite their
beſt

---

* Pſal. cxix. 130.   † Id.   ‡ Amos iii. 3.

beft endeavours, to profecute a meafure, concerning which they hold oppofite opinions, the one approving, and the other condemning : no, furely ; they mult firlt underftand one another, before they can act in concert.

Human authorities are alfo on our fide. The gene rallity of fenfible writers appear to hold this fentiment, that fociety is formed by confent. One may be mentioned, inftead of many, who fpeak to the fame purpofe. " We underftand by fociety" fays he, " the confent of two or more perfons in the fame end, and the fame means requifite to obtain that end ; wherefore, while fuch confent lafts, there is fociety. And fo foon as they who had formerly confented in the fame end and means, begin to propofe and purfue each his own end, that fociety is broke and diffolved."*

PROPOSITION V.

Departure from former laudable attainments, is a great evil, feverely threatened in the Holy Scriptures ; and that for which every one, who is guilty, muft be accountable to the Righteous Judge of all the earth.

The Spirit of truth affures us, " It had been better for them not to have known the way of righteoufnefs, than, after they have known it, to turn from the holy commandment delivered unto them." † Once enlightned, and having openly profeffed the truth ; they cannot now plead the excufe of ignorance ; they ftand felf-condemned, in the prefence of God, and before the world : their cafe is exceedingly dangerous.

This is one of the great and atrocious evils, for which God often threatened, and at laft feverely punifhed his ancient Ifrael. By the mouth of his prophet Jeremiah, he takes particular notice of their former attainments ; and he marks their departure from them, in language of the ftrongeft reprehenfion. They were once highly efteemed of the Lord, for " The kindnefs of their youth, the love of their efpoufals, and their going after him in
the

* Turnbull's Heineccius, Vol. 2. p. 10. † 2 Pet. ii. 21.

the wildernefs, in a land that was not fown. Ifrael was holinefs unto the Lord, and the firſt fruits of his increafe." But, on account of their apoſtacy, they were thus challenged, " What iniquity have your fathers found in me, that they are gone far from me, and have walked after vanity, and are become vain?" In JEHOVAH's difpleafure, they are told, " My people have committed two evils : they have forfaken me the fountain of living waters; and hewed them out ciſterns, broken cifterns, that can hold no water." To convince us that the difeafe was epidemical, that all ranks, from the throne to the cottage, were involved in the apoſtacy, and that backfliding in the ſtate, as well as in the church, is condemned and feverely puniſhed by God, we are told, " As the thief is aſhamed when he is found, fo is the houfe of Ifrael aſhamed, they, their kings, their princes, and their prieſts, and their prophets." The evil ſhall not go unpuniſhed; they muſt be accountable for the tranfgreffion: " Thine own wickednefs," faith the Righteous Judge, " ſhall correct thee, and thy backfliding ſhall reprove thee : know, therefore, and fee, that it is an evil thing and bitter that thou·haſt forfaken the Lord thy God."*. That divine injunction, " Whereto we have already attained, let us walk by the fame rule, let us mind the fame thing," † alfo proclaims the truth of the propoſition; and may be juſtly confidered as having for its object, every commendable, and fcriptural attainment, whether in civil, or religious fociety. Nor can it be refufed, that, the Redeemer's folemn warning to the church of Sardis, is full and pointed to our purpofe : " Remember," fays he, " how thou haſt received and heard, and hold faſt, and repent. If, therefore, thou ſhalt not watch, I will come on thee as a thief, and thou ſhalt not know what hour I ſhall come upon thee." ‡

---

* Jer. ii. 2, 3. 5. 13. 26. & 19th verfes.   † Phil. iii. 16.

‡ Rev. iii. 3.

THEY, who confent unto the unrighteous deeds of others, are chargeable with guilt, as well as the principal actors.

This is a maxim held facred, in all well regulated courts of judgment, amongft men. *Socii criminis*, or accomplices in the guilt, are juftly confidered as objects of the law; and punifhable for their confenting, and being aiding to the crime, though they may not have been the actual perpetrators thereof. Hence libels ufually ftate, " That fuch and fuch perfons have been guilty actors, or art and part: have concurred, or been aiding and affifting in the wickednefs fpecified."

The propofition likewife receives countenance, from the Oracles of truth. There the defpifers of the divine law are fharply reproved, not fimply for the more direct acts of fin, committed by themfelves; but alfo for confenting to the wicked deeds of others: " When thou fawelt a thief, then thou confentedft with him, and haft been partaker with adulterers." * What is faid, concerning thefe two atrocious evils, will hold with refpect to any other fin whatever. Confenting unto any fin, or doing what neceffarily involves an approbation of it, muft ever be reckoned criminal, in the fight of God. It is recorded, to the infamy of Saul of Tarfus, in his ftate of non-converfion, that when the proto-martyr Stephen was flain, " Saul was confenting unto his death." † Though it doth not appear, that he took any active part in the perpetration of the deed. And, as a beautiful contraft of his conduct, it is fpoken to the lafting honour of Jofeph of Arimathea, a member of the Jewifh Sanhedrim, that when the reft confpired againft the Lord of glory, and agreed to have him put to death, " He had not confented to the counfel and deed o them." ‡ He exonered his own confcience, by openly declaring his difapprobation of their procedure.

The

* Pfal. l. 18.   † Acts viii. 1.   ‡ Luke xxiii. 51.

The words of an infpired prophet, on this fubject, are very remarkable, " The Lord," fays he, " fpake thus to me with a ftrong hand, and inftructed me, that I fhould not walk in the way of this people, faying, Say ye not, A confederacy, to all them to whom this people fhall fay, A confederacy." * Approve not their evil counfels, confent not to their unrighteous deeds, neither hearken unto their enfnaring advices. The exprefs injunction of Heaven is, " Thou fhalt not follow a multitude to do evil; neither fhalt thou fpeak in a caufe to decline after many to wreft judgment." † Here we are commanded, not to fuffer ourfelves to be influenced by the voice of a majority, in a bad caufe; we are pofitively forbidden, to decline after them, or give our confent to their unrighteous determinations.

PROPOSITION VII.

THERE are two general kinds of fubjection, to fuperior power; that which is paffive or conftrained, dictated by imperious neceffity, on account of the afcendency which the exifting power hath obtained over the fubject; and that which is voluntary, deliberate, and confcientious, arifing from a lawful moral relation, between the fuperior and the inferior; which relation, among thofe who have the power of free agency, and enjoy the Word of God as a " lamp unto their feet and a light unto their path," muft ever be formed on rational and moral principles, or conditions, otherwife the authority can never bind the confcience of a moral agent.

It will not, furely, be refufed, that there is a ftriking difference, between the fervitude of the bond-flave, who reluctantly fubmits to the ftern authority of his haughty lord, finding himfelf obliged, contrary to his will, and oftentimes beyond his proper ability, to ferve with rigour, all the days of his life, without any juft recompence for his labour; and the voluntary obedience of the hired fervant, who enters into his mafter's fervice, in virtue of a mutual paction, plainly ftipulating what,

in

* Ifa. viii. 11, 12. † Exod. xxiii. 2.

in general at leaſt, is the work to be done, what ſhall be the term, and what the conditions of the ſervice. In the one caſe, the connection of maſter and ſervant is founded in cruelty and injuſtice; in the other, the relation is formed by mutual conſent. The one maſter hath no legal claim at all on the obedience of his ſubject; the other hath a juſt title to conſcientious obedience, natively reſulting from the paction, between him and his inferior. In the former caſe, man is treated either as a criminal, or as one of the brutal creation; in the later, he is conſidered as a reaſonable being, and free agent. In both the caſes, indeed, the things done by the ſervant may often be materially the ſame; yet formally viewed, as clothed with all its qualifying circumſtances, the ſubjection yielded is ſpecifically different. From the one obedience is extorted, by the mere dint of ſuperior, and, as to him, irreſiſtible power; while the other voluntarily obeys, in conſequence of a rational agreement, between him and his ſuperior. If all this be admitted, as reaſon certainly ſays it ſhould; then the diſtinction, marked in the propoſition, cannot, conſiſtently be refuſed.

The inſpired Apoſtle evidently favours the diſtinction, when he ſays, " Ye muſt needs be ſubject, not only for wrath, but alſo for conſcience' ſake." * Theſe words, indeed, ſuggeſt, and it is freely granted, that in the ſame caſe, the ſubjection may be of a mixed kind, partly paſſive or conſtrained, and partly voluntary; i. e. the ſubject, in yielding obedience, may be influenced, both by the conſideration of fear, and a ſenſe of duty. But what we contend for, at preſent, is, that theſe things are diſtinct, in their nature. If the ſubject, in obeying, have no other ſpring of action than imperious neceſſity, and the fear of a power, which he cannot poſſibly reſiſt; his caſe is ſurely very different from what it would be, did he feel the force of a moral obligation, upon his conſcience, in virtue of a lawful relation, between him and his ſuperior, and becauſe of JEHOVAH's command, to be ſubject unto the higher power; i. e. unto lawfully con-

* Rom. xiii. 5.

conftituted authority. Agreeably to this, we are led to diftinguifh between ufurped power, and lawful authority; between the wrong and the right manner of going to work, in forming the relation of fuperior and inferior; and between the terms, correfponding to thefe, paffive fubjeftion, and voluntary obedience for confcience' fake.

It is felf-evident that every moral obligation muft originally fpring from the authority of God, as the great Sovereign of the univerfe. And if fo, it would be exceedingly abfurd to fuppofe, that any human authority, affumed, on conditions directly contrary to his revealed will, fhould, notwithftanding, bind the confcience of his reafonable offspring; who are exprefsly required to take his Holy Word as the ftandard of their faith and practice.

PROPOSITION VIII.

SOCIETIES, or individuals, having once publicly, and folemnly vowed unto the Moft High God; and ftill, after the ftricteft enquiry, remaining fatisfied in their own mind, that their vows were fcriptural ; fhould ferioufly endeavour to act up to the true fpirit and intention of thefe vows ; and no power upon earth, nor any clafs of men, whether majority, or minority, in a nation, can ever poffibly diffolve the obligation.

The obligation of every confiftent and fcriptural vow, or religious covenant, which is much the fame, hath juftly been confidered as having fomething very facred in it. The reafon is obvious : the fovereign authority of JEHOVAH, is interpofed, in requiring this duty of his people; while his great and dreadful name is folemnly invocked, in thus obeying his will. " Vow, and pay unto the Lord your God," * is the unequivocal language of the divine law. The duty, indeed, is confef-fedly occafional; i. e. the confiftency, and propriety, of actually entering into formal vows, or covenants, arife, in a great meafure, out of the circumftances, in which the party is placed. But having once come into
thefe

* Pfal. lxxvi 11.

thefe circumftances; the law requires the proper improvement of them, in this manner. And the party, having endeavoured fo to do; the fame law requires the confcientious performance of that which he hath vowed. " When thou voweft a vow unto God, defer not to pay it; for he hath no pleafure in fools: pay that which thou haft vowed." † Hence, it is clear as noonday, that. ftrictly and properly fpeaking, the obligation always flows from the divine authority of the great Lawgiver. And therefore, though it be but a man's covenant; yet if it contain nothing, neither in matter, nor manner, but what is agreeable to the fpirit and fcope of the Holy Scriptures; its obligation fhould ever be held facred. It is not, we confefs, fimply confidered as the deed of men binding themfelves and their pofterity, that it affects our confcience; but formally viewed as the deed, which the Lord himfelf required to be done; as the vow, or covenant, which he commanded his people to make; and which, having been once made, he, no lefs exprefsly, commands them, confcientioufly, to fulfil. Thofe, therefore, who feel the weight of fuch obligations on their confcience, and are afraid, " After vows to make enquiry," ‡ may well be excufed.

Had I a proper opportunity of converfe with Mr. Fletcher, and the reft of our Seceding Brethren; I fhould wifh much to know, before we proceeded any farther, whether or not, they would grant the above general principles. To me it is a matter of no confequence whether they reckon them in point, or foreign to the purpofe; providing that they only allow them to be juft and true, in themfelves. If they do; I feek no other *dita*, in reafoning the matter, between them and us: but if they refufe any, or all of them; I fhould like to hear their objections, with the reafons and illuftrations of them. Meanwhile, till thefe appear, I hope, that I fhall now be allowed to take the propofitions for granted. Accordingly, aided by them, I fhall venture a few remarks, on the feveral fections of Mr. Fletcher's Defence.

ANIMAD-

† Eccl. v. 4.   ‡ Prov. xx. 25.

ANIMADVERSIONS, &c.

I AM extremely forry to find, that the very Title-page of our opponent's Performance affords room for animadverfion. It runs thus: " The Scripture-Loyalift defended, from unfair and falfe reafoning: with a refutation of falfe gloffes impofed on feveral paffages of the Holy Scriptures : and a detection of falfehoods, calumnies, mifreprefentations and contradictions." Surly-looking epithets, indeed! Here the prejudices of the reader are evidently befpoke, before-hand. His humours and paffions are addreffed, rather than his judgment and confcience. It was furely time enough for Mr. Fletcher to have given thefe names, to his opponent's arguments, after he had brought them to the bar, fairly tried them, and proved them to be falfe. Then, indeed, with fome appearance of reafon, he might have deduced it, as a neceffary inference, from the full and clear proof which he had led, that Mr. Steven's reafonings deferved no better names than thefe. But Mr. Fletcher's mode of procedure, is by no means candid; nor will it be eafy for any man to fhow, that his Title-page breathes a chriftian fpirit, or exhibits an inclination, to compofe differences. Mr. Steven goes to work in another manner. He, as every modeft difputant fhould, gives the fame names, which his opponent himfelf had given ; and, accordingly, entitles his Letter, " Anfwers to twelve Queries." It would have been equally eafy for him to have faid, " Anfwers to twelve Sophiftical Quibbles." And, in doing fo, he would have trode exactly in the fame path with Mr. Fletcher, as every perfon, capable of comparing without prejudice, muft fee at once ; but he has not thought it proper to do fo. And, I hope, neither will his furviving brethren : for unlefs we mean fairly to combat the reafoning, and candidly meet the arguments of our oppofers, with chriftian temper; it would be much better to drop the pen altogether.

ANI-

In this section of the Defence, the complaints against the Letter are, " Copiation; having as the scope, not to refute the doctrine taught by the Loyalist, but to combat the doctrine of paffive obedience and non-refiftance; indulging in paffion, invictive, and railing accufations; flooping below the good fenfe of a fcholar and divine, by mentioning country-clatters; miftaking the difpute between Seceders and the Reformed Prefbtery; making an Eraftian appeal; and artfully concealing the point in debate." †

If by copiation be meant, advocating the fame caufe which is ftated and defended in the Teftimony, and its Vindications; and, in fome few inftances, ufing, fubftantially, the fame arguments, though always ftated and illuftrated, in the author's own way, except where he profeffedly quotes, in fo many words; if this be all that is meant by copiation; nothing other was ever intended; nor could ever the author of the Letter, without it, have written, rationally, and confiftently, upon the fame fubject, on which others had written before him. But if by copiation be underftood, as the word feems rather to import, a fervile imitation of others, and tranfcribing, almoft word for word, from their books, without apprizing the reader; it is hoped, that Mr. Fletcher himfelf, upon fecond thoughts, will find, there is not the leaft fhadow of any fuch copiation, from beginning to end of the Letter; nor has he been able to produce a fingle inftance, in fupport of the charge. But might not our friend have fpared this reflection? confidering that he himfelf often writes the fame things over and over, in a very fervile manner. A ftriking inftance of which the attentive reader will find, by comparing the 6th Section and Conclufion of the Loyalift, p. 49. and 52. 2d. Edit. with the Conclufion of the Defence.

Mr.

† Def. p. 5,—11.

Mr. Fletcher affects to be very much perplexed, about the general fcope and defign of the Letter. He hefitates whether it has any determinate fcope, but if it has, fuppofes it to 'be, " To combat the doctrine of paffive obedience and non-refiftance." p. 6th. And again, "To prove that the Britifh Government is unlawful, and therefore fhould be difowned." p. 13. But there is not the leaft ground for hefitation in the matter. The intention of the Letter is clear as noon-day; namely, To anfwer Twelve Queries, propofed by Mr. Fletcher. We fhall, no doubt, be told, if that be the defign; it is yet unaccomplifhed; the Queries ftill remain unanfwered. But concerning this, the judicious and unbiaffed part of mankind, after carefully reading both publications, muft think for themfelves. Meanwhile, it is eafy to perceive, that he who appears firft, in a controverfy, has the liberty of adopting what plan he thinks moft proper, for his performance; while he, whofe part it is to reply, muft necef-farily follow his opponent, into his various ftrong holds of refort. If, therefore, Mr. Fletcher be not pleafed with the general fcope of the Letter; if he complain, that the true ftate of the queftion is miftaken; he cannot but fee, that he has himfelf wholly to blame. The Loyalift is, undoubtedly, attended, in his different motions; while, to illuftrate and prove his doctrine, he one while leads us to Egypt, the houfe of bondage and flavery; another while, to the land of Ifrael, under her own government, and her own kings, but in a ftate of awful degeneracy; now to Babylon, the fcene of tyrannical oppreffion, and impious infult; and then, to the land of Judea, while a province of the Roman Empire, under the yoke of the monftroufly wicked, and blood-thirfty Nero; and while, to crown the whole, he conducts us to Golgotha, and calls us to take a view of the fuffering Redeemer, humbling himfelf, in the room, and for the fake of his people, and thus becoming obedient to death, even the death of the crofs. * If the fub-

* Compare Sect. 1ft. & 2d. of the Scrip. Loy. with the correfponding anfwers in the Letter.

subjection, in general, which was yielded in the above cases, be not what we properly call, passive obedience and non-resistance; let the impartial reader judge. Now, if the Letter from Crookedholm had nothing to do with passive obedience and non-resistance, unless it had been addressed to Mr. Hobbs, * or some one of his stamp; it is surely difficult to see, what Mr. Fletcher had to do, to submit to the consideration of its author, these striking instances of passive obedience and non-resistance; unless he meant to defend the same cause, for which Mr. Hobbs contends. To deduce arguments, for enforcing and illustrating the doctrine of voluntary and conscientious obedience to lawful authority, from cases of the most abject slavery, is not, certainly, altogether consistent †.

Invective, passion, and railing accusation, are also charges against the Letter; and some extracts are given, to substantiate the charge. Meanwhile, it is confidently asserted, that "Seceders who fear God, will not render evil for evil, or railing for railing, but contrariwise blessing; and they will not offer strange fire on God's altar, lest they be consumed." ‡ It is evidently agreed, by both parties, that, in managing our disputes, the wrath of man is altogether improper, and can never work the righteousness of God. The only question is, unto what side the charge more properly belongs. Mr. Fletcher it seems, can see nothing of it in his Defence; and certainly the Author of the Letter saw, at least as little appearance of it, in his Pamphlet. And, indeed, it is very difficult for either the one, or the other, to judge impartially, in his own cause. The matter, therefore, must be, ultimately, referred to Him, who searches the heart, and tries the reins; and whose judgment is always according to truth. And, in as far as mankind are concerned, the impartial and discerning public must, and no doubt will, judge for themselves. It is but reasonable, however, that they should have the evidence on both sides. And as Mr. Fletcher has thought it proper, to give some extracts, from the Letter, as specimens

mens

* Def. p. 6.   † See Introd. prop. 7.   ‡ Def. p. 6, 7, 8.

mens of invective and railing accufation; he can have no
objections unto the producing of fome extracts, from the
Defence too, for a fimilar purpofe. This mode of proceeding, by collecting detached fentences, would certainly be very unfair, on either fide, were the defign to
afcertain the author's meaning; but this is not pretended; it is only to fhew the manner. The following expreffions will be found in the Defence.

 ' From your profound filence about the cardinal point
' in debate, it is probable that you have deferted the
' Reformed, and are come over to the Seceding camp;
' but it is far more probable, that *fave thyfelf*, is the
' parent of this filence.—I will not follow you through
' your whirlwind of noify and vain declamation, againft
' a fpectre of your own raifing.—The vain janglings
' and perverfe difputings of the Reformed Brethren.—
' This reafoninghasdriven Mr. Steven again to his dernier
' refort, to the ftrong-hold of magiftracy in the abftract.
' Scripture, reafon, and common fenfe, muft all bow
' to this metaphyfical idol.— Every man, poff-ffed of
' common fenfe, muft fee, that this comment is a bare-
' faced falfehood.—Advocates for error have great need
' of good memories, to prevent their falling into the
' mire of contradictions; and Mr. Steven's memory has
' greatly failed him.—This odd fenfe is fuch a grofs
' perverfion of a plain precept, it wears an afpect fo furly
' and forbidding, that you are afhamed of it, and there-
' fore laid it down at your neighbour's door; but it is
' now returned to you and the Reformed Prefbytery,
' as the right owners.—Much of your Letter confifts
' of manifeft contradictions, which would tempt one to
' think that it was written, not by one, but by feveral
' perfons not of one mind; and that it was put to the
' prefs by one, who had not ability to difcern, that one
' part of it was hoftile to another.—You might have
' feen, with your eyes half open.—You durft not look
' the feventh Query in the face, becaufe it hath a refpect
' to an article in the creed of the Reformed Prefbytery,
' which is exceedingly erroneous, or rather blafphem-
' ous; and therefore fhould never have been named

' amongſt Chriſtians. The diabolical article is this, &c.--
' Theſe ſayings have no more reſpect to the Query, than
' to the Popiſh doctrine of baptizing bells, and conjuring
' ſpirits.—Your anſwer to the eighth Query, conſiſts
' of falſehood and error, which are mighty weapons
' in your warfare, and always ready.—You durſt not
' attempt to prove your political principles from the
' Word of God, becauſe it would have been an attempt
' to prove, that rebellion, which is as the ſin of witch-
' craft, is authorized in the holy Oracles.' * To theſe
we may add a few bold aſſertions from the Loyaliſt.
' The Reformed Preſbytery are not found in the faith.—
' They are not going forth by the approven footſteps of
' the flock of Chriſt.—They do not reduce their own
' principles to practice. They are not going forth by
' the footſteps of the flock of Chriſt in Scotland in re-
' forming times.—And, they are not rendering to God,
' according to the benefit done unto them.' † If, agreeably to Mr. Fletcher's profeſſion, the above be the good,
which Seceders, who fear God, render for evil, the bleſ-
ſings, which they return, for the railing they receive;
what muſt their revilings be!—Ah! dear Sir, can you
calmly ſit down, lay your hand upon your breaſt, look
up with holy reverence to the throne of the omniſcient
God, and deliberately ſay, there is no appearance of
ſtrange fire, in any of the above extracts, no invective,
no railing accuſation; and, at the ſame time, affirm,
that the Letter from Crookedholm abounds in theſe?
No, ſurely; I hope our Friend will never run the awful
riſk. Alas! how readily do our treacherous hearts de-
ceive us! How blind are we to our own faults! Good
were it for us all; if we conſcientiouſly regarded our
Lord's advice, " Firſt caſt out the beam out of thine
own eye; and then ſhalt thou ſee clearly to caſt out
the mote out of thy brother's eye." ‡ Conſiſtent with
the high encomium, which Mr. Fletcher is pleaſed to
paſs upon himſelf and his brethren, I charitably hope
that there are many, among Seceders, as well as in other
ſocie-

* Def. p. 10. 12. 28. 36. 42. 62. 65. 80. 83, 84, 85. 92.

† Scrip. Loy. p. 20,—24.   ‡ Matth. vii. 5.

focieties of profeffing Chriftians, who truly "fear God;" but perhaps it might have faid as much for his modefty, if he had attended to the divine injunction, "Let another man praife thee, and not thine own mouth; a ftranger, and not thine own lips." * And he might certainly have exhibited fome better evidence, in the caufe, than the language, I am very forry, neceffity obliges me to call it, the taunting and fneering language of the above extracts.

As to the very loud complaint of "publifhing country-clatters," † though, in this inftance, it cannot be denied, that they were well-attefted ftubborn facts; the Author of the Letter, p. 4th. allows, that he "fhould have judged fuch things in themfelves altogether unworthy of notice;" and affigns his reafons why they are adduced by him. And indeed there can be very little propriety in defcending to notice fuch things, either on the one fide, or on the other. The openly avowed principles, of a body at large, are not to be meafured, by the dif-allowed practice of the individual. Meanwhile, the very ftrange conduct, which provoked to make this notification from the prefs, is certainly no lefs blame-able. And for my own part, I fhould be exceedingly happy to find all fuch practices, and the publifhing them unto the world, buried together in the fame grave; never more to be known amongft Chriftians.

In the 9th page of the Defence, the charge of an Eraftian appeal is introduced, with an air of remarkable triumph; while it is fuppofed that Mr. Steven has "betrayed the caufe of the Reformed Prefbtery into "the hands of its enemies." But the attentive reader will eafily perceive, that the author of the Letter from Crookedholm does not, ftrictly fpeaking, give up the caufe, neither into the hands of the Britifh Rulers, nor into any other hands: only, to ex-prefs his very ftrong conviction, of having common fenfe, and the ordinary reafon of mankind, on his fide, he fignifies, that he would not object, to the fubmitting of the controverfy, even to them, providing it were

fairly

* Prov. xxvii. 2.　　† Def. p. 8.

fairly ſtated; and riſks an opinion, that the iſſue would be favourable to his ſide of the queſtion. But whether or not, he might be miſtaken, in that opinion, were the experiment to be made, doth not at all affeƈt the merits of the cauſe. Meanwhile, it is truly aſtoniſhing, that the appeal, even ſuppoſing it had been aƈtually and formally made, ſhould be called "Groſly Eraſtian." *

Taking Mr. Fletcher upon his own terms; the queſtion is "about obedience to the lawful authority of the preſent Britiſh Magiſtrates." † If that be not a political queſtion; language has ſurely loſt its meaning. But what conneƈtion, the ſubmitting of a political queſtion; to political men, aƈting in their political capacity can have with Eraſtianiſm, very few, I apprehend, will ever be able to ſee. Is this indeed to give the keys of Chriſt's ſpiritual kingdom into the hands of the civil magiſtrate? Or, in other words, to allow him a direƈtive and authoritative power, in the diſcipline and government of the the church; reſerving, to the miniſters of religion, only a perſuaſive and conſultative power? Certainly not. When the Apoſtle Paul, on account of his ſtedfaſt adherence to the truths of the goſpel, was arraigned before the Roman Governor of Ceſaſea, and accuſed of ſedition, hereſy, and temple-profanation; it will not be refuſed that the queſtion partly reſpeƈted civil things; yet, taken complexly, one ſhould think, that it had at leaſt as much the appearance of a religious controverſy, as the queſtion about "obedience to the Britiſh Magiſtrates:" notwithſtanding, the Apoſtle, finding himſelf groſly abuſed, and wickedly impoſed upon, by his Jewiſh brethren, appeals the cauſe to Cæſar, the Roman Emperor; in expeƈtation that perhaps more juſtice might be got from him, though alſo an enemy to the religion of Jeſus. ‡ It is hoped that Mr. Fletcher will never think of bringing a charge of Eraſtianiſm, againſt that eminent miniſter of the New Teſtament; though, in a caſe ſtill more foreign to the ſubjeƈt, he brings it, with much confidence, againſt the author of the Letter from Crookedholm.

* Def. p. 10.　† Def. p. 9.　‡ Aƈts xxiii. xxiv. & xxv. Chap.

Having expreſſed a hope, that the Reformed Preſbytery would cenſure his opponent, for what is called his
" injudicious and Eraſtian appeal," Mr. Fletcher alſo
expeꝗts " That he will return to the good old Proteſtant
doꝗtrine, *That the ſupreme judge, by which all contro-
verſies in religion are to be determined, can be no other
but the Holy Spirit ſpeaking in the Scriptures.*" * But
is it really meant to apply this good old Proteſtant rule,
to the caſe in hand? Does Mr. Fletcher himſelf now
think, that the ordinance of civil magiſtracy, even in
a Chriſtian reformed nation, hath ſuch connexion with
religion, that a diſpute about it may be called, " A controverſy in religion?" Doth he now believe, that
magiſtracy is to be found in the Bible? Which muſt
unqueſtionably be the caſe; if a controverſy, concerning it, cannot be properly determined, but in the above
manner. But if this be truly his belief; it is difficult
to ſee, how he can, at the ſame time, teach, that " The
doꝗtrine of magiſtracy appointed in the written Word,
is pregnant with abſurdities." † Certainly importing,
that it is not appointed in the written Word. Now,
if it be a juſt obſervation, that magiſtracy is not appointed in the Word; I am afraid that all the Logic in
Chriſtendom will be inſufficient, to make the appealing
of a controverſy concerning it, unto political men, to
be " groſsly Eraſtian." The objeꝗts, about which alone
Eraſtianiſm is verſant, and concerning which it implies
an improper interference, are the Scriptural inſtitutions
of Chriſt, as the alone King and Head of his church.
Mr. Fletcher, ſurely, does not mean to make magiſtracy
one of theſe. Alas! how difficult is it, for even the beſt
of men, to maintain conſiſtency, eſpecially in the heat
of diſpute!

Concerning the ſtate of the queſtion, Mr. Fletcher
declares, that " The diſpute between Seceders and the
Reformed Preſbytery, is not about the nature of civil
government; nor about human laws, for the defence of
religious and civil liberty; but about obedience to the
lawful authority of the preſent Britiſh Magiſtrates." ‡

He

He complains upon his opponent for " profound filence about the cardinal point in debate." † And fuppofes, " No man can know from his Letter, whether he be a Britifh Royalift, or a French Democrate." ‡

- It feems we mult not be allowed to inquire, at leaft in managing the controverfy with our Seceding Brethren, concerning the kind of government, whether it be friendly, or unfriendly to the declarative glory of God, and the religious, or civil, liberties of mankind. But how we can, confiftently, argue the propriety, or impropriety, of yielding confcientious obedience, to any given authority, without examining into the nature, and properties, of faid authority, or confidering, upon what footing it is affumed; I freely confefs, it is not eafy for me to underftand. And it will, I apprehend, be extremely difficult for any man to fhew it; unlefs he mean to revive the juftly exploded doctrine, " That it matters not how the power hath been conftituted : if it exift, it hath a juft claim to my confcientious obedience, let the conditions, upon which it was affumed, be what they may." Subfcribing, indeed, to this language of abfolute power, and paffive obedience ; we need not much concern ourfelves about the kind of authority, to which our fubjection is required ; but otherwife, it is indifpenfibly neceffary. However, as the true ftate of the queftion, is a matter of very fpecial importance, in this, and indeed in every other difpute ; the readers patience is humbly craved, while we bring under review, the openly avowed fentiments, of both parties, expreffed in their own words ; that thus we may learn, how the controverfy ftands. And as Mr. Fletcher profeffes to teach, not a different, but the very fame doctrine, on the head of civil government, that hath been taught in the Seceffion fince its commencement ; we are warranted to confider the Affociate Prefbytery's " Declaration and Defence of their principles anent the prefent Civil Government," as expreffive of his and his brethren's fentiments ; fo long as they do not fee it meet to renounce that Declaration and Defence.

In

† Def. p. 10. || p. 11.

In anfwer to the queftion, What fort of kings the people of God are commanded to fear, fo as to own their authority, and fubmit to their juft laws, Seceders declare, " It is certain, that they are commanded to fear only fuch as are acknowledged by the kingdom they are in, while none elfe are kings with refpect to them. In the next place, It is as certain, that they are commanded to fear any whom that kingdom acknowledges as kings, and while they do fo." * In further illuftrating the text, Prov. xxiv. 21. they fay, " In a word, this text doth plainly teach, that the Lord's people, particularly, ought to fear all kings, who are acknowledged as fuch, by the kingdom they belong to; as there is no exception made here or elfewhere in Scripture." And in the next paragraph, " As there never were, nor could be, any kings acknowledged as fuch by a kingdom, but who adminiftered fome juftice; fo all the duty of particular fubjects, under the worft of thefe kings, is fufficiently comprehended in this command; as it binds them to acknowledge and fubmit unto their authority, in any lawful exercife of it, while the kingdom fuftains their government." † They allow it leaves them power to teftify againft the corruptions, and endeavour the reformation of the government. Speaking of men as having a natural inclination to civil fociety and government, their doctrine is, " Wherever they voluntarily conftitute or confent unto any form of civil government, under the rule of any particular perfons, whatever fin be in the circumftances of this their deed, with refpect to the government or governors which they conftitute or confent unto; yet the deed itfelf, or the fubftance of the deed, is always in confequence of, and agreeable to God's law; wherefore, their governors, as fuch and in the fubftance of the matter, are ordained of God, according to that law." ‡ Again, —" All thofe who are the ord'nance of man, or who have a conftitution by the confent of civil fociety, are to be fubmitted unto for the Lord's fake, or as having an inftitution from him." ⊦ Proceeding

ing in the explication of that submiffion, enjoined by the apoftle Peter, they alfo fay, " He orders them to yield fuch fubmiffion, without farther queftion, to every ordinance of man, every perfon in civil office by the will of fociety." † Concerning thefe precepts, in general, which require obedience to civil rulers, and which they had been confidering, as confirming their own principles, anent the government of the times, the fummary oblervation is, " As the precepts that have been explained, are a rule of duty equally toward any who are, and while they are acknowledged as magiftrates by civil fociety; fo they are and continue a rule of duty in this matter, particularly to all the Lord's people, in all periods, places and cafes.— There is not the leaft hint in all Scripture, that ever a time fhould come, or a cafe fall out, wherein the above precepts fhould not be a prefent rule." ‡

I fhould be very forry, to pervert our Brethren's words. But if the ordinary grammatical fenfe, and conftruction, are to be retained; I humbly apprehend, that the following conclufions, from the above extracts, are fair and neceffary.

1ft, That whatever may be the cafe in other departments of human life; yet in the formation of civil fociety, fixing its fundamental laws, and determining the conditions of bearing rule in it, even thofe who are favoured with the Word of God, as a lamp unto their feet, and a light unto their path, are not under any pofitive and indifpenfible obligation, to apply that ftandard. At leaft, though they fhould entirely lay it afide; and, according to their own fancy, organize their fociety, and inftal their rulers, on principles and conditions, in direct oppofition unto it; ftill their deeds are to be confidered as valid; and as juftly entitled to the practical approbation of every foul, within the territory. It will be objected, that owning the authority, even thus conftituted, doth not neceffarily imply an approbation of the evils in the conftitution, nor a fubfcribing to the propriety of thefe finful conditions, on which the crown

is

is held. Were thefe evils only verfant about fome accidental outfide-circumftances, or after-acts of maladminiftration; the objection might be allowed to have fome weight. But when thefe evils are particularly fpecified, incorporated into the very ground work of the conftitution, and pofitively ftood upon, as the fundamental conditions of rule; the cafe is quite altered. Then to fpeak of owning, in the proper fenfe of the term, the lawful authority of a ruler, who, in his regal capacity at leaft, hath no exiftence, but on the footing of folemnly fwearing adherence to certain fundamental laws of the kingdom, over which he reigns; and, at the fame time, pretend, that we heartily difapprove, and reckon ourfelves bound, in confcience, to teftify againft thefe very fame fundamental laws; if it be not a contradiction, it is certainly fomething remarkably like it.

2dly, That, even fuppofing the cafe of a nation, about to chufe their rulers, be ever fo plainly ftated, and the various circumftances of the cafe ever fo diftinctly afcertained; yet is it impoffible to fay, what would conftitute lawful authority, in faid nation, until the body politic, or civil fociety fignify their will. But if once the fanction of their confent, or of a majority among them, be given, that will legitimate the rule of any perfon over them; let the faid perfon be, otherwife, what he may, and the conditions of his advancement be as finful as you pleafe to fuppofe. For whatever Scripture-rules they defpife, whatever former attainments they relinquifh, or on whatever p inciples they go to work; ftill, it feems, the fubftance of their deed muft be confidered, as agreeable to the revealed will of God.

3dly, That, with refpect to civil government at leaft, the cafe of Heathens, who are totally ftrangers to the Word of God; and the cafe of Chriftians, who have the Bible daily in their hands, and who are exprefsly required to ufe it as the ftandard of their faith and practice, are fo very fimilar, that on whatever conditions the former may admit perfons to bear rule over

them,

them, confiflently with the knowledge they have; on the very fame conditions may the latter lawfully admit their rulers. For wherever, either in Heathen or Chriftian nation, the confent of civil Society can, once be obtained, that will legitimate the ruler's title to the throne, abſtracting from all other confiderations whatfoever. To whom much is given, of them, unqueftionably, more will be required, than will be of others; but though they fhould entirely diſregard what more is required of them; ſtill, it would appear, their deeds muſt be confidered as valid, and fanctioned by a " Thus faith the Lord."

4*tbly*, That even fuppoſing it fhould be freely granted, that human fociety ought to be formed, and the conditions of bearing rule in it fixed, by mutual confent, as to the majority, who happen to be of the fame opinion; yet the minority, who may happen to differ from them, have no alternative. With them there is no room for choice. Though, after uſing the beſt means of information in their power, they cannot, in judgment and confcience, approve of thofe fundamental conditions, on which the authority is held and exercifed; yet muſt they own it for confcience' fake. Without any hefitation, they muſt yield even to fuch things, as in their very nature, and by the common confent of mankind, neceſſarily involve a direct recognizing of the exiſting ruler's title. For thefe precepts, we are told, requiring fubjection to the higher powers, are to be applied, without farther queſtion, by all the Lord's people, in all places and cafes, where the will of the majority hath fet up rulers. As to that paffive fubjection, which doth not properly recognize the lawfulnefs of the title, it is altogether foreign to the fubjection in debate. And,

5*tbly*, That the reprefentatives of a nation, in organizing their fociety, and inveſting their rulers, may not only difregard the laws of Scripture, but alfo thefe correfponding fundamental laws of the ſtate, to which all ranks had folemnly fworn adherence before; and yet be at leaſt thus far blamelefs, that their public deeds while

while acting fo, fhould be practically fanctioned by every foul within the realm, in yielding confcientious obedience to that authority, which hath no exiftence upon any other footing. We fhall be told, The authority exifts by the will of human fociety; which is enough. Be it fo; but did not that will determine, that the authority fhould beheld and exercifed, on certain fpecified and ftipulated conditions; without fubfcribing, and adhering to which, it fhould be confidered as null and void. Whoever, therefore, acquiefces in the will, thus fignified, in doing fo, he neceffarily approves the object of its choice and determination; and will, I am afraid, be found chargeable with, fubftantially, the fame thing as the principal actor. If any fuppofe, that thefe conclufions are not fairly deduced from the premifes; it is hoped, they will not content themfelves with barely faying fo; but, by entering clofely into the merits of the caufe, will candidly fhew where the miftake lies, and how it is, that thefe things are not inferable from the doctrine of our Seceding Brethren. Till then, we muft be alowed to retain our opinion, that they are juft and neceffary confequences.

In oppofition to the doctrine of the above extracts, and the confequences which it neceffarily involves; the doctrine of the Reformed Prefbytery, on the head of civil government, is as follows,—" God Almighty, the Sovereign Lord of all things, hath, for his own glory and the public good, authorized and inftituted in his word the office and ordinance of civil government and governors, for the prefervation of external peace and concord, adminiftration of juftice, defence and encouragement of fuch as are, and do good, and punifhment of evil doers, who tranfgrefs either table of the law.— A due meafure of thofe qualifications which God the great lawgiver requires in his word, together with what other ftipulations, according to the fame unerring rule, a Chriftain people, who are bleffed with the light of divine revelation, have made the fundamental conditions of civil government among them, are effentially neceffary to the conftitution and inveftiture of lawful authority
over

over fuch a people. No other conftitution can be approved by God; nor anfwer the ends of the ordinance. —The conftituting of the relation betwixt rulers and ruled is voluntary and mutual. The lawful conftitution of magiftrates, is, by the mutual election of the people, and confent of thofe that are elected, with certain ftipulations, according to Scripture and right reafon, obliging each other unto the duty of their different ftations and relations." *

In this ftatement the following things are evidently implied, 1ft, That not only in other departments of human life; but alfo in the organizing of civil fociety, fixing its laws, and determining the conditions of bearing office in it, Chriftians, who are favoured with Divine Revelation, are indifpenfibly bound to apply it, as the ftandard of their conduct. 2dly, That when all the circumftances of a nation's cafe; with refpect to privileges, former attainments, and obligations; are carefully confidered, and tried by the unerring ftandard, it is poffible juftly to determine what are, and what are not, lawful conditions of invefting any perfon with civil authority over them; even previous to the declaration of the public will, by the reprefentatives of that nation. The conditions of inveftiture are either right or wrong, independent of their approbation, or difapprobation. 3dly, That our cafe, as a people bleffed with the light of Divine Revelation, and having once reached very high attainments in the ftate, as well as in the church, muft never be compared with the cafe of the Heathen, who fit in darknefs and in the region of the fhadow of death. 4thly, That as men are reafonable creatures, and as civil fociety fhould be formed, and princes admitted into office, by the confent, and free choice of thofe, over whom they are to rule; even the minority, in a nation, can never confiftently be forced, to fall in with meafures, which they do not in judgment approve. In fuch a cafe, they fhould be allowed, freely to diffent from the public deeds of the nation at large; nor ought any other weapons to be ufed, for reclaiming them, than thofe of

Scrip-

* Teftimony, p. 160. 4th. Edit.

Scripture and reafon; fo long as they conduct themfelves peaceably, and give no difturbance to fociety.
And, 5thly, That all national attainments, calculated to promote the glory of God, and the good of human fociety, ought to be held facred ; efpecially when
thefe attainments have been already openly approved,
incorporated into the fundamental laws of the ftate, and
adherence unto them folemnly fworn, by all ranks in he
kingdom. And although the majority fhould relinquifh
faid attainments, renounce their vows, and conftitute a
new fociety, on principles diametrically oppofite to the
former : their doing fo can never free the confcience of
the minority, difapproving of the new conftitution, and
fincerely wifhing ftill to adhere unto the ancient laws.

By carefully attending to the above contraft of the
principles, openly avowed by the refpective difputants,
it will be eafy to fee, how the matter ftands between
them. If all, who are favoured with the Scriptures, be
indifpenfibly bound to apply them, as the rule of their
conduct, even in their tranfactions concerning civil fociety ; Diffenters muft be right, in openly refufing their
confent to fuch public deeds of conftitution, and correfponding adminiftration, as not only fet afide that rule,
but in many, even fundamental articles, flatly contradict it : but if the Bible be indeed out of the queftion,
in thefe matters; Seceders may have fome plea for
their political principles. If conditions of vefting with
civil authority, as well as all other things in general,
be either right or wrong, in themfelves, and as determined by the Divine Law, independent of men's choice;
Diffenters may be juftified, in carefully inquiring into
the fundamental conditions of rule, in the nation where
they are, comparing thefe with Scripture, and former
good attainments, and either approving, or rejecting,
as they find them to agree, or difagree; yea, fo long
as they demean themfelve peaceably and inoffenfively,
no man can, confiftently, blame them, for refufing to recognize fuch authorities, as have no exiftence, but upon
anti-fcriptural conditions of advancement : whereas, if
there be no faying what is right, or what is wrong, on
that

that head, what is, or what is not indifpenfibly neceffary
to conflitute lawful authority, in any given circumftances, until the majority of the nation declare their will;
then Seceders may find it lefs difficult to fupport their
doctrine. If much fhall certainly be required of thofe,
to whom much is given, and if they who have finned
under the law, muft be judged by the law; it will be
hard to prove that Diffenters are wrong, in afferting,
that the cafe of the Heathen, who fit in darknefs, is not
parallel to the cafe of Chriftains, who enjoy the clear
fun-fhine of Divine Revelation, and that, therefore, there
can be no conclufive reafoning, from the one to the
other, even with refpect to the effentials of lawful civil
authority: but if the cafe be truly parallel, and the
very fame things fufficient to conftitute lawful authority,
in the one cafe, and in the other; then Seceders may have
much to fay, in their own behalf. If fociety fhould be
formed by mutual confent; where is the abfurdity of
teaching, as Diffenters do, that even the minority have
a right to be honeft recufants, when they find the fundamental laws of the new fociety, and the fixed conditions
of bearing office in it, contrary to Scripture, and to the
folemnly-ratified rules of the former fociety, unto which
they gave their hearty concurrence: but if rational
confent be unneceffary, and the minority fhould always
be obliged to yield, whether they can in judgment
approve or not; then Seceders may well blame us, for
refufing to fay, A confederacy, with the reft of the
nation. If we relinquifh former laudable and folemnly-
ratified, attainments, at our peril, and if thofe, who
afterwards confent, be guilty, as well as the firft tranf-
greffors; why are Diffenters condemned, for endeavouring, whereunto the nation hath already attained,
in the ftate as well as in the church, and whereunto
all ranks have fworn adherence, to walk by the fame
rule, and to mind the fame things? But if thefe attainments may be openly difregarded, and yet the nation be
at leaft fo far blamelefs, that we may fafely acquiefce
in thefe very fame public deeds of inveftiture which
involve, yea openly proclaim, the apoftacy; then we
need

need not be furprized, though our principles, on civil government, be every-where fpoken againft, and though our
Seceding Brethren be alfo loud in the cry. Once more,
if paffive obedience, or bearing the common public burdens of a nation, while no queftion is afked for confcience' fake, and while nothing, pofitively finful in itfelf, is required, be quite another thing, than free voluntary obedience, arifing from a properly conftituted
moral relation, between the fuperior and inferior, and
if this paffive obedience afcertain nothing, with refpect
to either the legality, or illegality, of the ruler's authority; Diffenters need not be fo much reproached, for
fuppofed inconfiftency, between their profeffion, and
their general, openly allowed practice, for as to the
difallowed practice of the individual, it is out of the
queftion, on both fides: but if there be indeed no fpecific
difference between the fubjection which may and muft
be yielded, in a cafe of conftraint, when thofe who are
permitted to rule over a people, becaufe of their fins,
have dominion over their bodies, and over their cattle
at their pleafure, and they are in great diftrefs, and that
fubjection which ought to be freely yielded ûnto the
Scriptural authority which we can, in judgment and
confcience, approve; then Seceders are in the right,
when they draw their arguments, for voluntary and
confcientious obedience unto lawful authority, from
cafes of paffive obedience and non-refiftance. It is
hoped, then, the intelligent reader will eafily perceive,
that the difpute, between Seceders and Diffenters, turns
properly upon the truth, or falfehood, of the general
propofitions, exhibited in the Introduction. If thefe
be admitted, as uncontroverted truths; every fentiment,
maintained by the Reformed Prefbytery, on the head
of civil government, will follow, as a juft and neceffary
confequence: whereas, if thefe can be proved to be
falfe; Seceffion principles, on that head, may be the
more readily vindicated.

Let us not, therefore, be any longer abufed, by laying
things to our charge, which we know not, and of which
we never entertained the moft diftant thought. The

F   quef-

queſtion is not about the ſtanding force of the many
Scripture-precepts, injoining obedience to the higher
powers. The binding obligation of theſe, in all periods
of the church, is freely granted, and ſtrenuouſly contended for, on both ſides: the difficulty lies, in the
practical application of them, to the proper object.
Neither is there any controverſy, concerning the evil
and danger of rebellion, againſt lawful authority: this
evil was never, in the leaſt, extenuated by Diſſenters,
more than by Seceders. Nor, if we would deal candidly
by each other, have we any diſpute, with regard to
the examples of the ſaints, either thoſe recorded in
the Scripture, or theſe of the martyrs, in later times;
as though we did not agree, whether they be a rule
unto us, or not. If they correſpond with the precept,
they are ſet for our imitation: if they do not, their
motto is, Beware of ſplitting on the ſame rock. This
doctrine, I hope, is firmly believed, and uniformly
taught, by both parties. But if once certain ſpecified
examples, like theſe of the martyrs in the late perſecution, be openly approved, on all hands, it may indeed
be a queſtion, To which principles do they ſhew the
moſt favourable aſpect? It is alſo foreign unto our
preſent conteſt, to inquire, what may, or what ſhould
be done by Heathens; who, not having the Scripture-
law, are a law unto themſelves? But let us be told,
what ſhould be done by us Chriſtians, amidſt all our
ſuperior advantages? Neither doth it any more properly concern this controverſy, to ſhew, what ſort of
government might have been born with, in a leſs perfect, and leſs enlightened ſtate of the nation: but, what
is requiſite now? Nor, laſtly, is the inquiry about
the propriety of demeaning ourſelves, peaceably and in-
offenſively, groaning beneath oppreſſive burdens, which
we cannot avoid; ſo long as no enſnaring queſtion is
put home to the conſcience, and while we have it not
in our power to make matters better. This Diſſenters
have uniformly endeavoured to do, ſince ever they were
a people. At no time, have they ever entertained the
remoteſt thought, of offering outward violence to any
man,

man, let his sentiments differ from their's, as much as they may. The weapons of their warfare are not carnal. But they wish to inquire, concerning such subjection, and such alone, as properly recognizes the title of rulers, holding, and exercising their authority, upon sinful conditions.

Let the dispute, then, be fairly stated. We have long enjoyed the Bible, as the complete rule of our faith and practice, in every department of life. We have reached high attainments, in state-reformation. These attainments have been incorporated into the fundamental laws of the kingdom. All ranks, in general, have solemnly sworn adherence unto them. Dissenters still feel, on their own conscience, the weight of that obligation. After mature deliberation, and diligently using every mean, in their power; they have no clearness to relinquish the former laudable, and fundamental conditions of bearing rule, in the kingdom of Scotland. The question, therefore, is precisely this, Whether, in such circumstances, it be really their duty, and they should still be obliged, to acquiesce in the public deeds of the nation; while forming a new society; advancing their rulers, on conditions, not only opposite unto, but destructive of the former; and while manifesting their loyalty, by such actions, as necessarily involve an approbation of the constitution, and recognize the justness of the ruler's title? Or, whether they should not rather be allowed to dissent, and manage their Testimony, under a public protestation, against these deeds; as they have actually done, first in the persons of their forefathers, and now in their own persons; especially so long as they still endeavour, notwithstanding their dissent, to live peaceably with all men, whether high or low, rich or poor?

If Mr. Fletcher chuse to meet us, on this ground; he may expect to be waited upon. But if he, or his brethren, mean to agitate questions, on other subjects, concerning which there is, evidently, no dispute between us; it is hoped, that they will be kind enough, to excuse some of us, at least, from seeing them again, in the field of this disagreeable contest.

Seem.

Seemingly refolved to make the poor Diſſenters appear as obnoxious as may be, Mr. Fletcher tells them, " A faying common with you, from prefs and pulpit, is, That the Britiſh magiſtrates are unlawful magiſtrates, and therefore all their commands are unlawful." † As our opponent hath not condefcended to mention either book, or page of the book, where this propofition is to be found; and as I do not remember ever to have met with it, in this form, either from pulpit, or prefs; it deferves no other attention, than what is due to all fuch manufactured doctrines. We have never made any objections to the government, without, at the fame time, affigning our reafons. If Mr. Fletcher chufe to combat thefe, and think, that he can overturn them; we are willing to liften unto him.

AND-MADVERSIONS on SECTION II.

In this fection, the chief complaint upon the Letter, from Crookedholm, is, that it brings a falfe, and un-proved charge, againſt the Loyaliſt; while it makes him to argue for paſſive obedience and non-refiſtance. " A quotation from the Loyaliſt," it is faid, " in which the doctrine of paſſive obedience and non-refiſtance is af-ferted, or necefſarily implied, would have done honour to Mr. Steven's underſtanding and honeſty." ‡ While it is fuppofed, that the Loyaliſt teaches the very op-pofite doctrine.

As Mr. Fletcher pofitively declares. that he is no ad-vocate for the flaviſh doctrine of paſſive obedience; it is but reafonable to give him credit for the affertion; and I fhould certainly be very forry to contradict him. At the fame time, that the pamphlet, entitled "The Scrip-ture Loyaliſt," produceth, generally, in fupport of the doctrine which it teaches, only fuch arguments, as ferve to plead the caufe of paſſive obedience and non-refiſt-ance,

† Def. p. 9.   ‡ p. 11.

ance, is clear as noon-day. The two great fources of argument, indeed, are faid to be Scripture-precepts, and, Scripture-examples. Both which, as rightly underftood, and properly, applied, will be readily acknowledged on all hands. But in applying general rules, the various circumftances, of given cafes, fhould furely be confider- ed. Had the Loyalift firft carefully confidered the pre- cious attainments of the nation, where the power exifts; defcribed the qualities of the power itfelf, by fhewing it to be properly conflituted moral authority; proved the conditions, on which it is given and received, to be fuch as are warranted, by the unerring ftandard; plainly pointed out the many good and important ends, for the accomplifhment of which it is exercifed; and then told us, that, having afcertained all thefe, the general rules muft now be applied; we fhould have frankly granted, that he was fpeaking to the purpofe. But if no other reafon be affigned, for the application of the pre- cepts, to the cafe in hand, than the bare exiftence of the power, the chiming over thefe words, "The powers that be;" the fum of fuch doctrine is neither more nor lefs, than this, "Be king who may; we muft be fubjects." The divine precepts are thus viewed and applied, in fuch a loofe manner, as makes them equally ready for the fervice of the abfolute tyrant, and of the lawful magif- trate. And what caufe that is calculated to plead, the impartial reader fhall be left to judge.

As to the inftances given, and the examples aduced, by the Loyalift, † they are, unqueftionably, on the fide of the fervile doctrine. They exhibit cafes of the moft pitiable, and abject flavery. They prefent to our view the people of God, as taught, indeed, to bear the op- preffive burdens, which were laid upon them. Taught, not by a confcience of duty, to lawful magiftrates, who had a moral right to rule over them; but taught, by the ftern law of neceffity, and the mere dint of fuperior power; from which they found it impracticable for them to extricate themfelves.

Was

† Def. p. 18,—21.

Was it not, with a witnefs, paffive fubjeftion, of this kind, which the fons of Jacob yielded to the haughty Egyptian monarchs, for feveral generations? The Lord himfelf charafterizes the powers, under whom they fhould groan. Says he to Abram, "Know of a furety that thy feed fhall be a ftranger in a land that is not theirs, and fhall ferve them, and they fhall afflict them four hundred years." * The hiftory verified the prediction. " The Egyptians made the children of Ifrael to ferve with rigour.—They made their lives bitter with hard bondage.—All their fervice wherewith they made them ferve, was with rigour.—Pharaoh charged all the people, faying, Every fon that is born, ye fhall caft into the river." † The Righteous Judge of heaven and earth himfelf evidently confiders Pharaoh as a very terrible fcourge, in the chaftifing hand of over-ruling providence. He views his chofen people, as fubjefted to a very fore punifhment, while under his arbitrary fway ; and therefore, he addreffes to Mofes this language of compaffion, " I have furely feen the afflidtion of my people which are in Egypt, and have heard their cry, by reafon of their tafk-mafters : for I know their forrows.—Behold, the cry of the children of Ifrael is come unto me : and I have alfo feen the oppreffion wherewith the Egyptians opprefs them." ‡

Of Nebuchadnezzar, the Babylonifh Monarch, who carried the Lord's people captive, this is the defcription,—" All people, nations and languages trembled and feared before him : whom he would he flew, and whom he would he kept alive, and whom he would he fet up, and whom he would he put down." ‖ In full confiftency with this abfolute defpotifm, we find him commanding to deftroy all the wife men of Babylon ; merely becaufe they could not tell, what it was fimply impoffible for any mortal to tell, without fome extraordinary revelation from heaven. § And, on another occafion, caufing public proclamation to be made to people, nations,

---

* Gen. xv. 13. † Exod. i. 13, 14. 22. ‡ Chap. iii. 7. 9.
‖ Dan. v. 19. § Dan. ii. 12.

tions, and languages, that they fhould fall down and
worfhip the golden image which he had fet up ; and that
whofoever would not fall down and worfhip, fhould the
fame hour be caft into the midft of a burning, fiery
furnace. * Both facred and human hiftory warrant us
to fay, that his fucceffors trode in much the fame path.
The fons of Jacob certainly beft knew their own real
fituation, under the foreign kings, who fwayed an arbitrary fceptre over them ; and who were the rod of God's
anger, and the ftaff of his indignation, for their punifhment. But, while they fat weeping by the rivers of
Babylon, their language, expreffive of their enflaved
condition, was, "They that carried us away captive,
required of us a fong; and they that *wafted* us required
of us mirth." † And, even in their, comparatively,
better fituation, under the Perfian Monarchs they ftill
find themfelves obliged to fay, "The kings, whom thou
haft fet over us, becaufe of our fins,—have dominion
over our bodies, and over our cattle, at their pleafure,
and we are in great diftrefs." ‡

As to Nero, under whofe tyrannical government
many of the primitive Chriftians lived, and during whofe
reign the Epiftle to the Romans appears to have been
written, the following account of him is given by an
author, whofe teftimony Mr. Fletcher cannot well refufe : "In the firft part of his reign," fays he, "he
behaved with fome decency and juftice. In the end of
it, he turned one of the moft tyrannical wretches that
ever breathed. He murdered his mother, and almoft
all his friends and principal fubjects.—He caufed burn
the city of Rome, and fung one of his poems at the view
of the flames.—He transferred the blame on the innocent Chriftians. Multitudes of them were apprehended;
fome were fewed up in the fkins of wild beafts, and torn
to pieces by dogs ; others were crucified ; others were
burnt in Nero's gardens, as nocturnal illuminations to
the city, while he, with great pleafure, beheld the fpec-
tacle from the window." ‖ Another account fays, "The
firft

* Dan. iii 4, 5, 6.   † Pfal. cxxxvii. 3.   ‡ Neh. ix. 37.
‖ Brown's Dict. of Bib. on the word Nero.

firſt who raiſed a general perſecution againſt the Chriſtians was the Emperor Nero, of whom Turtullian tells
the Gentiles; and, for the confirmation thereof, appeals to their public records; *We glory*, ſays he, *in ſuch
an author of our perſecution: any body who knows him,
may underſtand, that nothing but what is eminently good
could be condemned by Nero.* He was a prince of ſuch
brutiſh and extravagant manners, as their own writers
ſcruple not to call him a beaſt in human ſhape, the very
monſter of mankind." † A modern Author, ſpeaking
of him, and ſome other Roman Emperors, thus aſks,
and replies, " What was Nero, what Caligula? One
a bloody idiot, the other an inhuman madman; the firſt
like the ſecond, and both of them public robbers and
butchers. If their courſe of cruelties and oppreſſion
was government, ſo are plagues, tempeſts and inunda-
tions: but if their lives and actions were altogether
pernicious and deteſtable; the exterminating of ſuch
monſters from amongſt men, would have been a ſervice
to the whole race. Was Tarquin half ſo black and
odious? Yet who has ever blamed his expulſion? Was
the inſolence and tyranny of Tarquin the ordinance of
God?—What more right had Nero to take away the
lives of innocent men than any other aſſaſſin; what
more title to their fortune than any other robber; what
better right to ſpill their blood than any tyger? And
is it unlawful to reſiſt robbers, and aſſaſſins, and beaſts
of prey? Did the Almighty ever ſay of that beaſtly
tyrant, Touch not Nero my anointed, nor do his ruffians
any harm? Did Nero's ſtation leſſen or abrogate his
crimes?"

" What idea does it give of God, the Father of mer-
cies and of men, to repreſent him ſcreening that enemy
to God and man, as a perſon ſacred and inviolable;
and holding his authority from himſelf; the merciful
and holy Jehovah protecting an inhuman deſtroyer!
What more relation could there be between God and
Nero than between God and an earthquake, God and
a conflagration or maſſacre? The very ſound of the
phraſe

† Gillies' Hiſtor. Collect. Vol, 1. p. 7.

phrafe is fhocking to the foul! Is fuch reprefentation likely to make the name and nature of God amiable to men, likely to excite them to love and reverence him? Satan is faid to be delighted with the miferies and cala-mities of men; and to fuppofe that wicked being con-cerned for the fecurity of a tyrant, whofe office it is to debafe and afflict the human race, is natural and con-fiftent with his character : but I wifh men would not father upon the Author of all good fuch counfels and inclinations, as can only fuit the father of cruelties and lies." † Thefe fentiments, perfectly congenial with my own, I am happy to find expreffed, to much better pur-pofe, by this mafterly Writer, than they could have been by me. Mr. Fletcher will not, furely, reckon him a Doctor of our dubbing. He is an approver of the Britifh Conftitution, and dedicates his Book to Sir Ro-bert Walpole, the, then, Britifh Minifter; an evidence, that he was pretty high in favour. But when the mind is not warped by prejudice; the force of truth will often appear, where we would not fo readily expect it.

With regard to the example of our Saviour, in fuf-fering himfelf to be perfecuted, and fhamefully abufed, by the rulers of his time; it is, to the laft degree, aftonifhing, that ever any writer fhould think of drawing an argument from that, to prove the propriety of yield-ing confcientious obedience, to the powers that be; and yet deny, that he pleads the caufe of flavery ! Did Jefus fubmit himfelf to Herod, Pontius Pilate, and the rulers of the Jews, in virtue of any duty, which he owed unto them, as the minifters of God, who are a terror to evil doers, and the praife of them that do well? No, indeed; but it was their hour and the power of darknefs, and the authority which they exercifed over him, was wholly ufurped, tyrannical, and unjuft. In his fubmif-fion to them, he was placed in a fituation, in which none other ever was, nor ever will be. As the Surety of his people, he endured all the mal-treatment, and agonizing

fuffer-

---

† Gordon's Difcourfes on Tacitus, prefixed to his Tranflation of that Author. Dif. 5. Sect. 2. p. 53,—55. Fol. Edit.

fufferings, which they deferved, on account of fin.
Thefe fufferings had been typified and foretold, in the
Scriptures of truth. Yea, it had pleafed the Lord,
that the Saviour fhould be bruifed, and put to grief.
The defigns of Heaven muft, therefore, be accomplifhed.
It behoved him to fuffer thefe things; and enter into his
glory. From fuch confiderations it was, that he gave
his back to the fmiters, and his cheeks to them, who
plucked off the hair, and hid not his face from fhame
and fpitting. But inftead of requiring his people, voluntarily, to fujeƈt themfelves unto fuch treatment, and,
in fuch refpeƈts, to be the fervants of rulers; he gracioufly allows them to pray, " Deliver me, O God, out of
the hand of the wicked, out of the hand of the unrighteous and cruel man." † We fhall likely be told, " This
is not the fubjeƈtion intended by Chrift's becoming a
fervant of rulers: it refers to his examplary conduƈt,
in paying the tribute-money at Capernaum, and his
teaching to render unto Cefar the things that are Cefar's;
whereby he fhewed the propriety of obeying the powers
that were." ‡ With refpeƈt to the tribute demanded
at Capernaum, it is generally thought, that it was facred
tribute, given for the fervice of the fanƈtuary. But
whatever may be properly meant by it; this much is
certain, from our Lord's reply to Peter, that he confidered himfelf, as under no obligation to pay it; though
he did not chufe to quarrel with them, on that fubjeƈt.
As to his teaching, to give Cefar his due, even fuppofing, for a moment, the text fhould be underftood
as Mr. Fletcher would have it; yet to teach others
to be fervants of rulers, is one thing; and to become
himfelf a fervant of rulers, is another; fo that it can
never poffibly be proved, from this text, in what refpeƈt
our Saviour was a fervant of rulers. Befides, the
pious Mr. Henry, who is cited, with approbation, by
Mr. Fletcher, tells us, concerning Chrift's fubjeƈtion,
" This he fubmitted to, for our falvation." It is hoped
our friend himfelf will allow, that neither the paying
of

† Pfal. lxxi. 4. ‡ Mat. xvii. 24,—27. & xxii. 21. See Loy. p. 21.

of the tribute at Capernaum, nor the teaching to give Cefar his due, can, ſtrictly ſpeaking, be conſidered, as the procuring cauſes of our ſalvation, or as that, which, under the notion of a puniſhment, the Surety behoved to ſubmit unto, in his accompliſhing the work of our redemption. His agonizing and ignominious ſufferings, when pouring out his ſoul unto death, muſt ever be intended, when we ſpeak of the chaſtiſement of our peace being upon him. And, in theſe ſufferings, he might be viewed as a ſervant of rulers indeed; *i. e.* treated by them like a ſlave: inaſmuch as the Heathen and Jewiſh rulers, of that time, had the chief hand in conducting the bloody tragedy, and were the wicked, though overruled, inſtruments of his death; † even the death of the croſs; which was reſerved for the ſlaves, or bondſervants of Rome.

The attentive reader will eaſily diſcern the propriety of taking into conſideration the above inſtances of ſubjection to the ſeveral powers, which have been deſcribed. They are all produced, and ſtrongly urged by Mr. Fletcher as ſo many precedents, for our imitation, in owning the authority, and yielding conſcientious obedience unto the lawful commands, of the powers that be. ‡ For if he mean not ſuch objection, as properly recognizes the juſtneſs of the ruler's title; he ſpeaks not a word to the diſpute, between him and us. But as we have found all the above to be caſes of the moſt pitiable and abject ſlavery; the Loyaliſt's adducing, and keenly urging them, in ſupport of his doctrine, plainly proves him to be in the " hoſtile camp of abſolute power," whether he ever really intended it, or not. But if it ſhall ſtill be contended, that the above are not properly inſtances of paſſive obedience and non-reſiſtance, taught, not by a conſcience of duty to lawful moral authority, but by the ſtern law of neceſſity; might I be permitted to aſk, what theſe terms mean, or whether they have any meaning at all? For my own part, I freely confeſs, that after ſtriking the above from the liſt, I ſhould be altogether
at

† Acts iv. 26, 27.　　‡ Loy. 18,—21.

at a lofs to find a fingle inftance of flavery, in the whole
annals of hiftory, either facred, or profane. There is
not therefore, I apprehend, the leaft room for infinuating, that Mr. Steven could not produce a quotation from
the Loyalift, to fubftantiate the charge, of his pleading
the caufe of flavery. Mr. Steven hath very fully rea-
foned the matter; and made it abundantly evident, that
the general fcope, fpirit and tendency of the Loyalift's
argumentation, neceffarily lead us into the hoftile camp
of abfolute power. Yea, he hath cited feveral paffages,
in fo many words, largely animadverted upon them,
and fhewn that they fix the charge : as every impartial
reader, who hath paid proper attention to his Letter,
muft, at once, fee. †

I would charitably hope, that Mr. Fletcher's real fentiments are in oppofition to the obfolete doctrine of paffive obedience; and that it is only in the unguarded hour of
warm difpute, and flaming zeal againft Diffenters, that he
fays any thing to the contrary. But pray, for what reafon is it, that he deliberately produceth the above inftances of flavery in fupport of his caufe ? He will tell
us,—" The more defpotic the Roman Cefars," and the
other powers above mentioned, " were, the ftronger is
the argument for fubjection to the prefent Britifh Magiftrates.—If the Holy Ghoft commanded the Chriftians
at Rome to be fubject to Heathen Magiftrates, ought
not we to be fubject to Magiftrates who are profeffed, and
no doubt many of them true Chriftians ?" ‡ But not fo
very faft, dear Sir, if you pleafe. The conclufion will
only hold, upon the fuppofition, that you ftill intend the
very fame kind of fubjection. ⱡ If the argument ftand
thus, Seeing it was the duty of the Lord's people, in
the above cafes, and while they could not poffibly make
it better, to yield paffive obedience unto thofe powers,
who, for holy and wife purpofes, were then permitted to tyrannize over them ; much more is it our duty
now,

† See Mr. Steven's Anf. to Query 5. Let. p. 80,—88. alfo p. 103, &c.

‡ Def. p. 28.   ⱡ See Prop. 7. in our Introduct.

now, while matters continue as they are, to yield paffive obedience to the milder Britifh rulers ; I know no ingenuous Diffenter, who will not readily fay, Amen. We certainly reckon it our duty to live peaceably and inoffenfively ; to fubmit to fuch things as are, in their own nature, lawful or innocent; and even, with as much patience as poffible, to bear the oppreffive burdens which may be laid upon us, while we cannot help it, and while thefe things are not required as teffaras of our loyalty, nor any enfnaring queftions put home to the confcience ; which is what I would underftand by paffive obedience, in cafes of neceffity. But let the argument be ftated thus, as indeed it is virtually done, in both the Loyalift and Defence : Becaufe the Lord's people, in the above cafes, yielded, as they neceffarily behoved to do, paffive obedience unto the powers, under which they then were ; therefore it is our duty, to own the authority of the prefent Britifh Magiftrates, as lawfully conftituted authority ; to which we owe allegiance and fubjeΩion, for confcience' fake ; it is apprehended, that then Mr. Fletcher's reafoning is by no means conclufive. Any perfon acquainted with the very firft rudiments of Logic, will eafily difcern the defeΩ ; and fee, that, in the progrefs of the argument, there is a fudden, and unexpeΩed tranfition, from one fort of fubjeΩion, unto another fpecifically different: Should our opponent complain, that we have here introduced a new term ; he fpeaks nothing about allegiance to the prefent government, when he pleads that we fhould own its authority and obey its lawful commands ; I would beg leave to reply, that to fpeak about owning authority, as lawful, and voluntarily obeying a power, as ordained of God, "loyalty to which is clearly taught in the Scriptures of truth, and rebellion againft which is as the fin of witchcraft;" and yet refufe that we owe, and ought to fwear allegiance unto it, will be found, I prefume, a much more glaring inconfiftency, than any, which have yet appeared, between the generally allowed praΩice of Diffenters, and the principles, which they maintain.

The

The quotations from the Loyalift, as we find them towards the end of this Section, † in order to fhew that he never was in the " hoftile camp of abfolute power," only ferve, after what hath juft been proved upon him, to confirm more ftrongly Mr. Steven's obfervation, " that he is like the watermen, who fet their face one way, and row another." ‡

Mr. Fletcher is glad to find Mr. Steven adopt, and exprefs in ftronger terms than even he himfelf hath ufed, the doctrine of the Loyalift, with refpect to obedience, or fubjection, in things lawful, to thofe of a different religion, or even to tyrants. ‡ If his joy be fincere; why fhould it not be indulged? Peaceable fubmiffion, in cafes of neceffity, to things lawful in their nature, even under the greateft tyrants and ufurpers, is a matter concerning which, fo far as I know at leaft, there never was any difpute, between Seceders and Diffenters. But fubjection of this kind, is one thing; and owning lawful authority, is another. There is not, therefore, the fmalleft ground for that challenge, with which the Section concludes, " How comes it to pafs, that the very fame doctrine," taught in the Letter, when " taught by the Loyalift, is injurious to truth, and to the civil and religious privileges of men?" It has this tendency, Sir, only when you introduce it to prove, that every government, under which fuch fubjection is, or ought to be, yielded, muft, confequently, be confidered and owned as a lawfully conftituted government; or, in other words, the moral ordinance of God, appointed for his glory, and the happinefs of human fociety, and which is clearly entitled to our voluntary obedience, for confcience' fake. If you only contend for the fubjection itfelf, as expreffive of the Chriftian's peaceable and inoffenfive deportment, under any government, and at the fame time grant, that this kind of fubjection doth not at all affect the queftion, about properly owning the authority, or recognizing the juft title of thofe, to whom it is yielded; we have no difpute, on that head. You may

† Def. p. 12,--14.   ‡ Let. p. 110.   ‡ See Def. p. 13, 14.

may fafely, without running any hazard of being contra-
dicted by us, exprefs fuch fubjection, in terms as ftrong
as thofe in the Letter, or even ftronger, if you pleafe.
But the attentive reader cannot fail to difcern, and
Mr. Fletcher himfelf knows, perfectly well, that while
Mr. Steven is fpeaking of this fubjection, in ftrong
terms, he, all along, pofitively refufes, and fhews how
it cannot be, that it hath any connection with owning the government, under which it is yielded. or that
it can ever be confidered as any proof, that the authority, requiring it, is lawful.

ANIMADVERSIONS ON SECTION III.

SCRIPTURE precepts and examples; the conduct of
the martyrs, under the late perfecution; and the duty
of praying for wicked rulers, are the principal objects
of attention, in this Section.

Concerning the precepts and examples, it is hoped,
that the reader will remember what hath already been
faid. † From them all, in general, Mr. Fletcher thus
infers, If it was the duty of the faints to be fubject,
in fuch and fuch cafes, then; much more is it our duty,
now, when matters are comparatively on a better footing. Agreeably to what was faid above, the force of
the reafoning is eafily admitted, and militates nothing
againft Diffenting principles; providing that only the
fame kind of fubjection be required now. But the
queftion is, Did the fubjection that was either enjoined,
or actually yielded, even then, properly imply a recognizing of the ruler's title? Did it neceffarily involve
an approbation of the conditions, upon which he occu-
pied the throne, and fwayed the fceptre? An idea altogether infeparable from the owning of any authority, in
the ftrict and proper fenfe of the term. Did it, in all
the

† See the foregoing p. 40,—47.

the cafes, comprehend folemn allegiance to the exifting power, as the lawful authority, appointed by
God, for his own glory, and the good of human fociety?
Would it have been warrantable for the Lord's people,
poffeffing their own land; having the benefit of Divine
Revelation; already brought forward to very high attainments, in ftate-reformation; engaged, by public
vows and former fundamental laws of the kingdom, to
preferve thefe attainments; and now acting voluntarily,
in their national capacity, all which were in the cafe,
at the Revolution, 1688; would it, I fay, have been
warrantable, in thefe circumftances, to have chofen,
for their rulers, fuch perfons as the Egyptian, Baby-
lonian, and Perfian monarchs, or the Heathen Roman
Emperors, efpecially fuch as Nero? " No fuch thing,"
Mr. Fletcher will reply, " was ever either faid, or intended." If fo; then the producing of thefe inftances,
to afcertain the lawfulnefs of the authority, in our times,
and circumftances, and to enforce obedience, and allegiance unto it, as fuch, muft be entirely foreign to
the fubject. Our opponent will probably grant, as his
brethren have done, before, that the reprefentatives
of the nation, at the Revolution, in relinquifhing the
reformation-attainments, and in adopting quite new
and oppofite conditions of advancement, to places of
power and truft, acted very far wrong, † " but now the
powers that be, are actually raifed to their places, by
the body politic, or majority of the nation, they rule
by the confent of the far greater part of the fubjects;
you are but a very fmall and inconfiderable minority;
you ought, therefore, to live peaceably, and fubmit
to every thing which is innocent and lawful." So fay
Diffenters alfo; and their avowed principles never led
them to think, nor to fay otherwife. But, meanwhile,
they are not fond of being forced, to approve fundamental laws, and conditions of government; which,
after all the means of information they can ufe, ftill
appear to them, diametrically oppofite, both to Scripture,
and

† Declar. & Def. of Prin. p. 50, 51.

and reformation-attainments; nor do they wiſh to do any ſuch things, as neceſſarily imply that approbation: which is what they properly mean by diſowning the government; and not perſonal hatred of the exiſting rulers; diſturbing human ſociety; propagating their principles, by open force; or joining, in the wicked counſels, and inconſiſtent meaſures, of ſuch as may be diſpoſed to raiſe ſeditious tumults, and appear in open rebellion againſt thoſe, who, for the preſent, fill the places of power and truſt; for theſe are things to which they have ever ſhewn a juſt and ſtrong averſion.

As to the litigated paſſages of Scripture, which are again brought under review, in this Section; it would be quite idle, to travel the ſame ground, over and over. If the candid inquirer can ſhew the miſtake, I ſhall be happy to receive his information, and to ſtand corrected by him; but to me it appears, that the amount of what Mr. Fletcher hath here laid upon them, is plainly this, " After all, which the Loyaliſt can find, in the Letter from Crookedholm, he ſtill retains his former ſentiments, with little or no variation; and, if the reader chuſe to let him ſpeak for himſelf, it will be ſeen that he hath expounded theſe paſſages right." Accordingly, quotations are often given; and he is frequently called forward, to ſpeak in his own behalf. Much of this trouble, I ſhould think, might have been ſaved, by ſimply deſiring the reader, carefully to look over the Loyaliſt again. In like manner, it might, at preſent, ſuffice, in reply, after what hath been already ſaid, to deſire the ſame reader, carefully to look over the interpretations given by the Reformed Preſbytery, in their Teſtimony, and by Meſſ. M'Millan and Steven, in their reſpective Letters; and then judge betwixt them, as he may find cauſe. A number of human authorities, indeed, are likewiſe mentioned by Mr. Fletcher; but this was alſo done by Mr. Steven, on his ſide of the queſtion. And to theſe we might now add a ſmall pamphlet, entitled, " Sacred Politics." The Author of it, whoever he is, cannot ſurely be ſuſpected of being a Scotch Diſſenter. It would rather appear, from his Preface, that he knows

H   nothing

nothing of their exiſtence, or at leaſt of their principles; and yet he explains the litigated paſſages nearly, if not exactly, in the ſame manner, in which they do:

But even ſuppoſing we ſhould grant Mr. Fletcher the benefit of all his expoſitors, on theſe texts; he will perhaps, find it very difficult to prove, that the ſubjection, for which they plead, implies any thing more than that paſſive obedience, which may and muſt be yielded, under any exiſting government, having full power over a people, becauſe of their ſins. In the quotation from Pool are theſe words, "—Although Ceſar be an uſurper, yet God hath given you into his hands, you have owned him, by accepting his coin as current among you." * Pray, what other ſort of owning, or ſubjection, than that juſt mentioned, could it conſiſtently be ; or what more could even their paying of the tribute, ſuppoſing they were actually to do it, neceſſarily imply ? Was it their duty, formally and explicitly to recognize the title of an uſurper ? Certainly not : nor is it poſſible to believe, that our Saviour would ever have required of them any ſuch thing; as Mr. Steven has indeed clearly proved, by many ſtrong and concluſive arguments † ; which, very wiſely for his own cauſe, Mr. Fletcher hath been pleaſed entirely to overlook. In the quotation from Henry, it is ſaid, "—Some think, the ſuperſcription upon this coin, was a memorandum of the conqueſt of Judea by the Romans, *Anno poſt captam Judeam ;* and they admitted this too."‡ Does Mr. Fletcher, aided, as he ſuppoſes, by the pious Mr. Henry, mean to teach, that conqueſt furniſhes out a juſt title to regal authority over a people ? If he do ; in vain ſhall he ever afterwards refuſe, that he pleads the cauſe of ſlavery. It will be no ſalvo to ſay, that their conſent to wear his yoke, legitimated his authority ; for they were expreſly bound, by the law of their God, to chuſe one of a very different deſcription ; it could not, then, conſiſtently at leaſt, be a matter of voluntary choice, but of neceſſity. They might find themſelves obliged to ſubmit unto

Ceſar's

* Def. p. 15. † See Let. p. 89,—107. ‡ Def. p. 16.

Cefar's yoke, as a juſt puniniſhment for their ſins, and even ſuppoſing God had required them patiently to bear it, yet could they never be called to conſider it as a public good, or as a proper objeƈt of moral choice : a light, in which every lawful authority ought certainly to be viewed. If Mr. Fletcher ſhould grant, that the lawfulneſs of the authority in queſton is not aſſerted in theſe texts, nor has it any neceſſary conneƈtion with them, † I beg leave to reply, that no other ſort of ſubjeƈtion, ſuppoſed to be enforced by them, can in the leaſt militate againſt the declared principles of Diſſenters.

Mr. Fletcher maintains, that the ſenſe which the Reformed Brethren have given of Mattli. xxii. 21. is three-fold, and full of manifeſt contradiƈtions. " —The firſt," ſays he, " repreſents Chriſt as teaching, That tribute was neither due nor undue to Cefar. The ſecond repreſents him as teaching, That death was due to Cefar. And the third repreſents him as forbidding to give tribute to Cefar." ‡ I am truly ſorry that ſuch childiſh banter, for even charity forbids to give it another name, ſhould ever have dropt from the pen of one, claiming the honourable appellation of a goſpel-miniſter. Becauſe the Reformed Brethren, as he is pleaſed to call them, may find occaſion to make three, or, it may be, ſix, or even ſuppoſing it were ten, diſtinƈt obſervations, in order to aſcertain the true meaning of a paſſage of Scripture; does that ſay, that they impoſe ſo many different and contradiƈtory ſenſes upon it? If Mr. Fletcher were not determined, wilfully to pervert the language, and to diſregard the ſcope and conneƈtion of the explanation, given by his opponents; he would find it to be as much one, as that for which he contends. It is ſimply this, That, for holy and wiſe reaſons, which they particularly notice, our Saviour declined, as he did in ſeveral other caſes, to give any direƈt anſwer at all, unto the captious queſtion that was put, to enſnare him. Whether Cefar's claim to the tribute-money was juſt,

or

or unjuſt, he did not chuſe to ſay. But becauſe we find him, in another caſe, declining to comply with the requeſt of the man, who aſked him, to ſpeak unto his brother, that he might divide the inheritance with him;* does that ſay, he taught him, that the inheritance was neither to be divided, nor left undivided ? Becauſe he declined directly to anſwer the queſtion, concerning the woman taken in adultery; and, finding that none of her accuſers had condemned her, ſaid, " Neither do I condemn thee;" † does that ſay, he taught, that ſhe was neither to be condemned, nor uncondemned; neither put to death, nor ſuffered to live ? No ſuch thing. Neither can Mr. Fletcher's allegation, concerning the Reformed Preſbytery's interpretation of Mat. xxii. 21. be more conſiſtently admitted.

Though obliged himſelf ſometimes to defend his doctrine by very abſtract reaſoning, as Mr. Steven has clearly proved againſt him;‡ yet our friend Mr. Fletcher, hath a mighty ſtruggle, for ten or eleven pages together, with thoſe harmleſs antagoniſts, " Magiſtracy in the abſtract," and " A practical ſubmiſſion to God's ordinance, even while it is not veſted in the perſon of any human adminiſtrator." ⊹ Seemingly reſolved to fight neither with ſmall nor great, but with theſe terms ; he chimes them over, one or other of them, twenty or thirty different times, in this Section. Had Mr. Steven been properly aware, that he had to do with an opponent, who was determined to diſregard his ſcope, run away with detached expreſſions, and torture every unguarded word, in the moſt unmerciful manner; he might probably have ſeen, that the term, " practical ſubmiſſion," in the caſe before us, was not the moſt happily choſen. He does not indeed appear to have been taken altogether at unawares ; for, in his Letter, he grants, that he may very readily " be corrected in words improperly choſen,—and thoughts improperly expreſſed ;" and expects, that " Occaſion may likewiſe be taken,

to

---

* Luke xii. 13, 14   † John viii. 3,—11.   ‡ Let. p. 45.
⊹ Def. p. 18,—25.

to drefs up thefe in fome hideous form, and then combat
the man of flraw with great pomp." † How exactly is
the expectation realized, in this Section of the Defence!
To every candid, and unprejudized reader, however,
Mr. Steven's meaning is perfectly obvious. It is evidently this, that Chriftians may not only, in their judgment and confcience, heartily approve of civil rule, and
proper fubordination, amongft mankind; but, in their
daily practice, and in all their civil tranfactions, may
actually demean themfelves, in an orderly, decent and
becoming manner, according to the true fpirit and defign of every well regulated magiftracy; even where,
for the time being, there is no formally organized legiflature, or any civil magiftrates, as yet, actually inftalled
into the office. Without granting this, it will be very
difficult to fee, what either is, or can be done, in cafes
of important, neceffary, and, if you will, glorious revo-
lutions; when the throne is abdicated, or vacated, by
fome means or other; when there is a total interregnum;
and, for the time being, not fo much as a regency. At
fuch times, it is allowed, great diforders have often
happened. But it would bear very hard upon the characters of our fellow-men to fay, that even in fuch cafes,
none could be found, who manifefted, even by their
practice, a proper regard to civil order, or good government, amongft mankind.

But after all, I humbly apprehend, that Mr. Fletcher
fhould fhew a little more lenity to magiftracy, even ab-
ftractly confidered: that mode of expreffion hath certainly been ufed, in treating various other fubjects; by men,
as famous in their generation, and of as diftinguifhed
abilities, I fuppofe, as any amongft either Seceders or
Diffenters; while they do not appear to have been
blamed, by the beft linguifts, or the fevereft critics of
their time. And what, if Mr. Fletcher himfelf fhould
ftill need the aid of that very idea, which he fo exceed-
ly reprobates. He allows, that the paffage, Rom. xiii.
1.—7. "—Contains an exhortation to be fubject to civil
rulers,

† Let. p. 129.

rulers, with motives to enforce the exhortation." * The motives muſt certainly be ſuch as theſe, " their being the miniſters of God for good, a terror to evil-doers, and the praiſe of them that do well." For he alſo allows, that " Rulers in the third verſe, and God's Miniſters in the ſixth, are an explication of powers in the firſt verſe." † Conſequently, it is ſtill the ſame power, to which we are required to be ſubjeƈt, on pain of condemnation ; and which is particularly deſcribed, in the ſame paſſage. But after you have ſtript Nero, the Roman Emperor, of all the amiable charaƈters here given ; and, if the above account of him ‡ be juſt, as I believe it is, he certainly, eſpecially towards the end of his reign, did not aƈtually poſſeſs ſo much as one of them ; you will have, if not magiſtracy in the abſtraƈt, at leaſt as abſtraƈt a ſort of magiſtrate, as imagination itſelf can form. He muſt be conſidered, merely, formally, and abſtraƈtly, as a magiſtrate; without any regard to the lawfulneſs of his title, his real charaƈter, his aƈtual adminiſtration of the government, or the ends for which he ſwayed the ſceptre. So far was he from being a terror to evil-doers ; that he was himſelf the very head and chief of them. And, inſtead of being a praiſe to them who did well ; he was the violent perſecutor, yea, and bloody murderer, of ſuch as did well, in reſpeƈt of both civil, and religious well-doing. ‖ Yet to this very abſtraƈt magiſtrate indeed, or, which amounts to the ſame thing, to this Emperor, ſimply conſidered as a magiſtrate, without regarding either the nature, the rule, or the reaſon of his aƈtual government, the primitive Chriſtians, it ſeems, could, conſiſtently enough, yield praƈtical ſubmiſſion.

" If this abſtraƈt ſenſe," ſays Mr. Fletcher, viz, that againſt which he contends, " be true, it muſt be invariable; for the meaning of Scripture doth not change with the times." § To this we add our hearty Amen; and it makes much for our purpoſe. The abſtraƈt ſenſe

is

is certainly invariable, namely, That civil magiſtracy is a precious ordinance, appointed by God, for his own glory and the good of human fociety. This is a truth clearly taught, by the Holy Spirit, in the paſſage before us : and it is a truth, which will remain invariable, to the end of the wórld. It is no lefs invariably true, that when and wherefoever, we can find civil powers, clothed with the amiable charaƈters ; and, by their government, anfwering the important purpofes, particularly fpecified in the paſſage, they ought to be confidered as the powers ordained of God ; to whom we owe fubjeƈtion, for confcience' fake. There is no lawful authority, as the original word properly fignifies, or moral power of this kind, at any time, or in any part of the world, but it is of God, as the great fountain from which it proceeds. All the powers, of this defcription, which are to be found amongſt men, in whatever period of time, and in whatever place, are to be owned, and fubjeƈted unto, as exprefly appointed of God ; for the promoting of his own glory, and the happinefs of mankind. Thefe we confider as uncheangeable truths ; evidently taught, in this paſſage of Scripture.

And, by the by, it is humbly fubmitted, to the judicious and candid reader, whether there be any violence done to that mode of expreſſion, " the powers THAT BE," by giving this turn to the paſſage; or whether it be not even more natural, fimple, and eafy, than the cramped interpretation, which confines it to the powers, then exiſting at Rome; as though the words had run in this manner, " The powers which, at the prefent moment, aƈtually exiſt in Rome, are ordained of God."— Mr. Fletcher himfelf, it is hoped, will allow, that thefe two expreſſions, " There is no power," and, " The powers that be," are equally extenfive, in their meaning and application. "Every fchool-boy can tell, that the words," in both cafes equally, ʻʻ are in the prefent time." But when it is faid, " There *is* no power," whether is this the meaning, There is no power, at prefent exiſting in Rome; or is it rather, There is no lawful power or authority, neither at one time nor another,

ther,

ther, nor in any place whatfoever, but it fhould be
confidered as of God? And if this fenfe fhall be admitted here; by what rule of interpretation is it, that the
other phrafe, " The powers that be," fhould be underftood in a more limited fenfe? Is it not ftill the fame
fubject, which is faid to be " of God," and " ordained
of God?" When our Saviour fays, " There *is* no man,
that hath left houfe, or brethren, &c. —but he fhall
receive an hundred fold—"; † we all know that the word
is in the prefent time; and yet we muft certainly underftand him as fpeaking in general terms, with refpect
to all periods indifcriminately: as much as to fay,
There is no man, at any time, or in any place, who
bears the amiable character, but he fhall receive the
gracious reward. That our Saviour meant thofe of his
own time, as well as thofe of other times, providing
they anfwered the defcription given, is freely granted.
And, upon the fame principle, it will not be refufed,
that the Apoftle means all powers, anfwering to the
characters which he gives; but ftill it muft remain to
be determined, whether Nero be one of thefe. That
he exilled in his time, is known; but that he anfwered
his defcription of the lawful power, is much, and juftly,
queftioned. When the Preacher fays, " There be juft
men, unto whom it happeneth according to the work
of the wicked: Again, there be wicked men to whom
it happeneth according to the work of the righteous;" ‡
every one muft allow, that he is fpeaking, in general terms, concerning what happens in the world, at all
periods; without confining his attention to the men of
his own time, more than to thofe of other times. It
would appear, therefore, that, after all the mighty
noife we have heard, concerning thefe two little words,
" That be," as though they were, " A ferpent by the
way, an adder in the path,—a ferpent that muft not be
roufed, but upon our peril;" ‡ they do not give the
fmalleft countenance to that interpretation, which makes
the infpired Apoftle to mean thofe very bloody and
tyran-

† Mark x. 29. 30.   ‡ Eccl. viii. 14.   ‡ Loy. p. 15.

tyrannical powers, then actually exifting in Rome. An interpretation which receives all its plaufibility from playing on the bare found of the word BE; without properly attending to the well-known phrafeology of Scripture. I am not alone, in this opinion, concerning the fcope of the paffage before us. The words of the great Mr. Herle, who was Prolocutor of the Weftmin-fter Affembly, after Dr. Twifs, are, exprefsly to the fame purpofe. "The powers here are faid to be or-dained of God, and verfe 2d. to be the ordinance of God.—The Apoftle fpeaks in the general, without ap-plication to the Roman or any other, but on the con-trary, it is ftood upon, that he intends his precept of a lawfully called Magiftrate." *

It is one great beauty of Divine Revelation, that it contains ftanding rules, for directing the faith and prac-tice of mankind, in all the diverfified fituations, and re-lations of life; whether, for the time being, they may actually fill fome of thefe relations, or not,. Whenfo-ever they come into the circumftances defcribed; then the rule, given for the direction of their conduct in fuch circumftances, properly applies. And, indeed, this idea is infeparable from a complete and univerfal ftandard; by which truth and error, fin and duty, or right and wrong, are afcertained, in every fuppofable cafe, and the line of diftinction fo fairly drawn, that no one, when he finds himfelf actually in fuch a cafe, fhould be at any lofs to know the path of duty. This being the cafe, there is no abfurdity, in teaching what are the refpective duties of magiftrates, and fubjects, although, for the prefent, there fhould not be any formally organized legiflature; or none properly deferving the honourable name.— JEHOVAH himfelf taught the fons of Jacob, how they were to regulate their conduct, with regard to their princes, and alfo how their princes were to behave, hundreds of years before they had a king. ‡ Query, Were thefe precepts of any ufe to Ifrael, at that time?

The

---

† Differtations, p. 126. 131.

‡ Deut. xviii. 14,—20. comp. Acts xiii. 20.

I

The Martyrs, with whom Seceders wifh to claim kindred, were no ftrangers to the doctrine, of owning Magiftracy in the abftract; and, at the fame time, difowning thefe human adminiftrators, in whom the power was vefted, for the time being. " —I charge you," fays James Stewart, in his laft fpeech, " to beware of mifconftructing my fufferings, and faying that I was fuffering for difowning of authority, and declining of judges; for it is not fo, I being a Prefbyterian in my judgment, and owning both magiftracy and miniftry, according to the word of God, and as he hath ordained them : but· if Charles Stuart's authority be according to the word of God, I am miftaken. If he be exercifing his power, to the terrifying of evil-doers, and the encouraging of them that do well, I die in an error." †

Mr. Fletcher goes on : " According to this abftract fenfe, Paul has exhorted all the churches of Chrift, from his own day to the end of the world,—to fubmit practically to the ordinance of Magiftracy in itfelf." ‡ Certainly he exhorted them, always, to confider Magiftracy as an ordinance of God; and to demean themfelves accordingly. If providence fhould ever order their lot under fuch magiftrates, as he defcribes; let them carefully remember, that even the religion of Jefus, notwithftanding all the unjuft reproaches caft upon it, exprefsly requires, to own and obey fuch, as the minifters of God. for good. And, if their lot fhould fall even· where there are no lawful magiftrates, none but tyrants and, ufurpers; yet ftill let their behaviour be harmlefs and blamelefs, as the fons of God, without rebuke, in the midft of a crooked and perverfe generation; plainly manifefting, by every part of their conduct, that they are the friends of order, and that it is their conftant ftudy, to lead quiet and inoffenfive lives, in all godlinefs and honefty. We have the vanity to think, that even fuppofing the Apoftle, to have exhorted the Chriftians after this manner; there is nothing either ridiculous, or abfurd, in it. Meanwhile, were we

to

† Cloud of Wit. p. *(mihi)* 220.   ‡ Def. p. 19, 20.

to treat Mr. Fletcher's comment, as he doth ours; how eafy would it be, to turn his artillery againſt himſelf: " If that ſenſe, which makes the Apoſtle enjoin ſubjection to Nero, be true, it muſt be invariable, for the meaning of Scripture doth not change with the times: accordingly, Paul has exhorted all the churches, from his own day to the end of the world, practically to ſubmit, not to lawful magiſtrates in general, but to Nero and the other exiſting powers at Rome in particular." Even a babe in knowledge may ſee, that the concluſion is juſt as fair, in the one caſe, as it is in the other. Though it is frankly acknowledged, that none of them are genteel. And this ſhould not have been mentioned here, but merely for the purpoſe of ſhewing Mr. Fletcher, what he might expect; were others to take the ſame freedoms with his expreſſions, which he takes with theirs. Becauſe Mr. Steven taught, that it was practicable for Chriſtians, in the conſtant tenor of their lives, to ſhew themſelves friends to civil order, even where there was not, for the time, any organized legiſlature; did he, therefore, teach, that they were not to be ſubject to lawful magiſtrates, even when they could obtain them? No ſuch idea ever entered into his mind, or was ever expreſſed by him.

" Mr. Steven," ſays his opponent, " uſes another argument, p. 54. for ſupporting his abſtract ſenſe, and it is drawn from 1 Cor. vi. 1.—But the two paſſages are by no means parallel. In the one, Paul exhorts the Romans to obey magiſtrates; and, in the other, he reprehends the Corinthians, for going to law with one-another about trifling matters, which might eaſily have been decided by friendly arbitration. The conſideration of theſe paſſages as parallel, is a manifeſt perverſion of the meaning of both; for it makes the enjoining of a duty, and the reprehenſion of a ſin, to be one and the ſame thing." † The reader will be pleaſed, to look into the quoted page of Mr Steven's Letter; and he will ſee, that he ſpeaks not a ſingle word, neither about an abſtract

† Def. p. 22, 23.

ſtract ſenſe, nor about theſe paſſages being either parallel, or unparallel. He views the one as helping to explain the other. And aſſigns his reaſons, why he
conſiders the Apoſtle as reprehending the Corinthians,
not ſimply for going to law with thoſe things, which
might be ſettled by friendly arbitration ; but for going
to law, on whatever pretence, before infidel and incompetent judges. This laſt he conſiders as the thing, upon
which the Apoſtle chiefly reſts his reproof. And, therefore concludes, that we cannot conſiſtently with this,
ſuppoſe him to mean ſuch infidel and incompetent judges
as theſe, in that other paſſage, Rom. xiii. 1.—6. inaſmuch as the higher powers there mentioned, inſtead of
being ſuch as we ſhould ſhun, are plainly ſuch as even
Chriſtians are bound in conſcience to own ; whoſe tri-
bunals they ſhould ever reverence ; and whom they
ought always to conſider as appointed of God, for the
very purpoſe of puniſhing evil doers, and defending
thoſe who do well. That the enjoining of duty is one
thing, and the reprehenſion of ſin is another, can eaſily
be diſcovered ; nor is it much more difficult to ſee,
agreeably to what Mr. Steven here ſuppoſes, that both
thoſe Scriptures which enjoin duty, and thoſe which reprove ſin, may be of ſpecial uſe for making us underſtand more clearly, what is ſin, and what is duty ; who
are the miniſters·of God, and who are not. But the
attentive reader will, at once, ſee, that our friend, Mr.
Fletcher, in place of ever touching his opponent's arguments, or deigning to drop a ſingle word, in reply to
any of them : frames, and anſwers, a queſtion entirely
new, and concerning which, there never was any diſpute between him and us, namely, Whether theſe two
paſſages of Scripture, above mentioned, be parallel, or
not ?

While Mr. Fletcher, in his gloſſing this paſſage,
1 Cor. vi. 1.—8. refuſes Mr. Steven's view of it, and
excludes the conſideration of the magiſtrates before
whom, and of their incapacity, on account of their being
Heathens, and Idolaters ; I am afraid, that he will not
receive much countenance from the beſt Expoſitors ; of

whom

whom he, fometimes, feems rather difpofed to boaft. Guyfe, Pifcator, Pool's Synopfis, Henry's and Pool's Continuators, with many others, take all particular notice of the Heathen Magiftrate's incompetency, to act in thefe matters, as that upon which the reproof turns; allowing at the fame time, indeed, that the Corinthians are alfo reproved for going to law at all, about thefe differences, which might be fettled otherwife. Guyfe, in giving the contents of the chapter, fays, "The Apoftle cautions the Corinthians againft going to law one with another, efpecially in Heathen courts, ver. 1.—8. And in the paraphrafe on ver. 1.—" Is it not a rafh, unneceffary and unwarrantable venture,—for any of you who have a matter of controverfy with a Chriftian brother about civil affairs, to enter immediately into a law-fuit againft him, and try it in a litigious way before Heathen magiftrates, who are avowed enemies to Chriftianity;—and from whom impartial juftice to its profeffors is not ordinarily to be expected." Which interpretation exactly correfponds with that which Mr. Steven hath given.

In oppofition to Mr. Fletcher's fcheme of interpreting Rom. xiii. 1,—7. Mr. Steven had objected, "That it entirely ftrips the martyrs, under the reign of Charles II. and James VII. of any countenance from Scripture precept or example, for their conduct in rejecting and difowning their authority." † Mr. Fletcher replies, "If this objection had been duly pondered, it would never have feen the fun. The conduct of the beft of men muft ftand and be judged at the bar of Scripture.— But, according to this objection, the Scripture muft ftand, and be judged at the bar of human conduct.— Idolatry is forbidden in the fecond commandment; but how abfurd would it be to conclude, that it is not forbidden, becaufe this fcheme of interpretation gives no countenance to the conduct of Ifrael, who made a calf in Horeb, and worfhipped the molten image! Murder is forbidden in the fixth commandment; but

how

† Let. p. 88.

how unreasonable would it be to infer, that it is not forbidden, becaufe this fcheme of interpretation gives no countenance to the conduct of David in killing Uriah the Hittite with the fword of the children of Ammon." *

When prejudice takes the place of candour; nothing will pleafe. Mr. Thorburn had taught, that " We have a better and furer rule to direct our moral conduct, than the practice of the belt and holieft men that ever lived." And that " Neverthelefs when Scripture examples are pretended to be agreeable to Scripture precepts, they mult be taken notice of †." As much as to fay, When examples are agreeable to the precept, they fhould be followed; but when they are not, they cannot be confidered as any rule to us. Doctrine, one fhould think, not very unlike to that which Mr. Fletcher himfelf here teaches, when he fays, that " The conduct of the belt of men mult ftand, and be judged at the bar of Scripture. — And fhould commentators walk by the conduct even of confeffors and martyrs as a rule, they would make void the law of God by their expofitions." ‡ Immediately, however, the Loyalift, citing as his proof, that very part of Mr. Thorburn's book juft mentioned, cries out, " That the Reformed Brethren have rejected the approven examples of faints in Scripture." † On the other hand, knowing that the conduct of the martyrs, under the reigns of Charles II. and James VII. had already been tried, at the bar of Scripture, and got an honourable teftimony, to the propriety of it, from both Seceders, and Diffenters; Mr. Steven juftly takes its agreeablenefs to the Scripture-precept, at prefent, for granted. And then he charges his opponent's interpretation of Rom. xiii. 1,—7. with this abfurdity, That it ftrips the martyrs of any countenance, from Scripture-precept and example, for their conduct, accufing them of wantonly throwing away their lives, by carrying their principles beyond what was required from men,

in,

---

* Def. p. 30, 31. † Vindiciæ Mag. p. 104.
‡ Def. p. 30. ‡ Scrip. Loy. p. 76.

in their fituation; for if, agreeably to Mr. Fletcher's
doctrine, fuch bloody and perfecuting tyrants as Nero
were to be owned, and fubmitted to, for confcience' fake,
unqueflionably, upon the fame principle, fuch bloody
and perfecuting tyrants as Charles II. and James VII.
fhould alfo have been owned, and fubmitted unto.
The neceffary confequence, from which is, that the
martyrs, under thefe reigns, muft have died in an error;
while, in place of owning, they rejected the then authority.   Let Mr. Fletcher therefore fhew how he is con-
fiftent with himfelf, in paffing very high encomiums on
thefe martyrs' conduct; and, at the fame time teaching
fuch doctrine, as unavoidably leads us to this conclufion,
that inftead of refifting and ftriving againft fin, they died
refifting the power which was ordained of God, and to
which they fhould have been fubject, for confcience'
fake.   Meanwhile, it is clear as noon-day, that it is
only the good, and approved examples, of thefe renowned worthies, which Mr. Steven, all along, confiders as
deferving our regard, and imitation.   And to this, we
fhould have thought, Mr. Fletcher himfelf need not have
objected; feeing his own doctrine is, " That the approven examples of the faints in Scripture are as much
the rule of our duty, as the precepts of the moral law." *
But ftill Mr. Fletcher muft find fault; if it fhould be,
for teaching exactly his own doctrine, and therefore,
he now complains upon his opponent, as though he
taught, " That Scripture is to ftand, and be judged at
the bar of human conduct."   Yea, by introducing thefe
two examples of very atrocious wickednefs, Ifrael's grofs
idolatry and David's very aggravated murder, he evidently fuppofes him to have taught, that all the faints'
examples, whether good or bad, were fet for our imitation.   But of this Mr. Steven never dreamt, nor is
there the remoteft hint of any fuch thing, neither in his,
nor in any of his brethren's writings.   It is prefumed,
Mr. Fletcher himfelf, after ferious confideration, will
find, that thefe two inftances of very fhameful blunders

in

* Scrip. Loy. p. 20.

in profeffing faints, and the honourable conduct of the
late martyrs, in refifting unto blood, ftriving againft fin,
are at leaft as far from being parallel, as the two fore-
mentioned paffages of Scripture, Rom. xiii. 1,—7. and
1 Cor. vi. 1,—8. Why then is the invidious comparifon
infinuated; and conclufions drawn, from the one cafe
to the other? Mr. Fletcher certainly knows, that, if we
would be candid, there is no proper difpute between
Seceders and Diffenters, concerning the duty of following thofe, who through faith and patience are inheriting
the promifes.   Such examples, as are agreeable to the
divine law, we fhould carefully imitate; and fuch as are
not, we fhould no lefs carefully, fhun, though fet by the
beft of men. In this we are all agreed.—But Mr. Steven
is fpeaking about the true fpirit, and tendency, of thofe
examples, which had been uniformly approved by both
parties.   And it is truly aftonifhing, that ever Mr.
Fletcher could allow himfelf, to pervert his words, in a
manner fo exceedingly ungenteel, that even charity,
which thinketh no evil, can fcarcely cover. If controverfies, amongft the profeffing friends of Chrift, are ftill
to be thus managed; " Tell it not in Gath, publifh it
not in the ftreets of Afkelon; left the daughters of the
uncircumcifed triumph!".

Mr. Fletcher labours, and indeed it much concerns
him, to have it eftablifhed, that even the martyrs, under
the two Royal Brothers, though they rejected the ecclefiaftical fupremacy; yet did not properly difown the
civil authority of thefe princes. " It was not," fays he,
" the civil, but the ecclefiaftical ufurped authority, in
and over the church, which they rejected and difowned,
'as their faithful teftimonies plainly declare." *   If he
mean to fay, They did not refufe, that thefe princes,
notwithftanding all that they had done, in violating the
fundamental laws of the kingdom, had ftill a juft title
to the Britifh throne, and were actually clothed with
fuch lawful authority, as ought to be owned, and fubmitted to, for confcience' fake; their own words, it is
prefumed, will prove, that he is miftaken.

With

* Def. p. 32,—36.

With refpect to thefe few renowned champions, who concurred in the Queen's-ferry Paper, and who ex-exprefsly renounced all allegiance to King Charles II. Mr. Fletcher, indeed, hefitates much about the propriety of their conduct, in this matter; † and no wonder, for he cannot poffibly approve of it, but at the expence of entirely ruining his own caufe. They were but a very fmall minority; and yet they rejected the then exifting powers. But he produces, from the fpeeches of other martyrs, fome extracts, which he confiders as making more for his purpofe. And it is truly aftonifhing, that even Mr. Cargil's fpeech finds a place among thefe. The following part of it is cited by Mr. Fletcher. "As to the caufe of my fuffering, the main is not acknowledging the prefent authority, as it is eftablifhed in the fupremacy and Explanatory Act. This is the Magiftracy that I have rejected, that was invefted with Chrift's power." But does our opponent fuppofe, that fuch as truly refpect the memory of thefe noble martyrs, will read only a part of their fpeeches, and ftop fhort in the midft of a paragraph. The very fame Mr. Cargil, in the fame fpeech, yea, in the fame paragraph too, hath thefe exprefs words, "—Seeing it (the fupremacy) made the effential of the crown, there is no diftinction we can make, that can free the confcience of the ac-knowledger, from being a partaker of this facrilegious robbing of God. And it is but to cheat our confciences, to acknowledge the CIVIL POWER; for it is not civil power only that is made of the effence of his crown: And feeing they are fo exprefs, we ought to be plain; for otherwife it is to deny our teftimony, and confent to his robbery." ‡ I am afraid, that Mr. Fletcher muft be found guilty, either of uncharitably fuppofing, that this venerable martyr knew not what he was faying, when, in fo many words, he declared, that the acknow-ledging even of the civil power, was but a cheating of the confcience; or elfe, of infulting his reader, by pro-ducing this fpeech, as favouring his fide of the queftion.

The

† Def. p. 34, 35.   ‡ Cloud of Wit. Edit. Glaf. 1779. p. 37.

K

The next in order, in the Cloud of Witneſſes, is Mr. Smith, ſtudent of Theology. In his ſpeech, he affirms, " —This is the main point, this day, in controverſy, upon which I was peremptorily queſtioned, and deſired poſitively to anſwer, yea, or nay, under the threatening of the boots, *viz*. Whether I owned the King's authority, as preſently eſtabliſhed and exerciſed? Which I did poſitively diſown, and denied allegiance to him, as he is inveſted with that ſupremacy proper to Jeſus Chriſt only. And who knoweth not, that at firſt he was conſtitute and crowned a covenanted king, and the ſubjects ſworn in allegiance to him, as ſuch, by the Solemn League and Covenant. — But the WHOLE of this pleaded-for authority, at preſent, is eſtabliſhed on the ruin of the land's engagements to God, and to one-another." † Still, indeed, the ſupremacy is particularly mentioned; not, however, as the alone thing which they rejected, while they owned the authority in other things; but as the formal reaſon why they diſowned the authority altogether. The king's authority is expreſsly mentioned, " as preſently eſtabliſhed and exerciſed." For they had ſenſe enough to diſcern, that, in any other view, it was a non-entity; the king had no other regal authority, neither to be owned, nor diſowned.

James Boig, alſo ſtudent of Theology, is next in the liſt. In his laſt teſtimony are theſe words,— " We could not own the authority as preſently eſtabliſhed, unleſs we ſhould alſo own the ſupremacy, which the king hath uſurped over the church; becauſe the ſupremacy is declared in their acts of parliament, to be eſſential to the crown; and that which is eſſential to any thing, is the ſame with the thing itſelf: ſo that, in owning their authority, we are of neceſſity obliged to juſtify them in their uſurpation alſo." ‡ Mr. Boig ſpeaks of the king's authority in general, under a diſtinct conſideration from the ſupremacy; yet he ſuppoſes it ſimply impoſſible to own the one without the other;

ſee-feeing the fupremacy was made effential to the crown. " Thefe chariots of Ifrael, and the horfemen thereof," did not, it feems, poffefs the penetration of fome, who claim the honour, of being their fucceffors; otherwife, they might have feen it abundantly confiftent, to own a civil government, not only as juft and lawful, but as the beft government under heaven ; without in the leaft owning that Prelacy and that Headfhip over the church, which are the very ground-work of the conftitution; and pofitively declared, by public deeds and laws of the nation, to be effential to the crown. † Poor Dif-fenter's, indeed, muft claim no kindred with thefe champions for civil and religious liberty; though they think exactly as they thought; namely, that it is impoffible to own any authority, in the ftrict and proper fenfe of owning and acknowledging, without, at the fame time, owning thefe things, which are made effential to the wearing of the crown, and fwaying the fceptre; and without which it is not allowed to do either the one, or the other, for a fingle moment, till the exifting fundamental conditions of rule be altered.

Robert Gray, another of thefe faithful witneffes, in a letter which he acknowledged to be his own hand-writ, and to which he ftill adhered, when he was interrogated before the Council, expreffes himfelf thus, "—In anfwer to that, about owning this tyrant in ecclefiaftic matters. I hope it is without all doubt and debate, with all the zealous exercifed Chriftians in Scotland, that he fhould not be owned at all in it.—And as for owning him in CIVIL THINGS, to me it is very clear, now as matters are

---

† In fixing the fucceffion to the Britifh Crown, at the Revolution; one article was, " That whofoever fhall hereafter come to the poffeffion of this Crown, fhall join in communion with the Church of England, as by law eftablifhed." This was made an effential condition of wearing the Crown. Judge Blackftone, in his Commentaries on the Laws of England, declares, " The king is confidered, by the laws of England, as the head and fupreme governor of the national church. — In virtue of this authority the king convenes, prorogues, reftrains, regulates, and diffolves all ecclefiaftical fynods or convocations." Thus far he. See Mr. Steven's Pofthumous Let. p. 41,—44.

are ftated, that he fhould not be owned."† It is obfervable, that he immediately afligns feveral reafons,
why he could not own him, even in civil things.

James Robertfon, who ranks in the fame honourable
lift, fpeaking of the king, in his laft fpeech, fays, " —As
to that which is fo much pleaded for by this generation,
his authority in civil matters, which as matters now
ftand cannot be given, neither will they have it without
the other : for, by their acts of parliament, they have
made them equally effentially to the crown : Likewife
there cannot be an authority without a foundation." ‡
This plain and honeft martyr wanted penetration to difcern, how an authority can, ftrictly fpeaking, be juft
and lawful ; while the fundamental conditions, upon
which it is held and exercifed, are pofitively finful.
He not only maintained, that the rulers would not have
the civil, without the ecclefiaftic authority ; but, that
the one could not, confiftently, be given, any more than
the other, as matters now ftood. But we need not un-
neceffarily fwell this pamphlet, by producing more inftances.

Let the reader carefully confult the Cloud of Witneffes, from beginning to end ; and he will find, that all
the martyrs, whofe fpeeches are there recorded, and who
fpoke of the king's authority at all, did, to a man,
totally reject the powers that were. Several of them,
as we have feen, fpoke profeffedly on the fubject ; and,
in fo many words, flatly deny the king's authority
altogether, both in civil, and ecclefiaftic matters.
Many others folemnly declared their adherence to
the Teftimonies of thofe, who had gone before, and
to the Sanquhar Declaration, the Queensferry-paper,
and other Deeds of that kind ; in which the exifting
powers were wholly rejected, and pofitively pronounced
tyrants. The number of thofe, who faid little or nothing on that fubject, was very fmall. And though
fome few, upon interrogation, gave fort of indirect anfwers; fuch as, " I own all authority, which is agreeable

to

† Cloud of Wit, p 229.   ‡ p. 244.

to the Word of God."—" I own them, as they are a
terror to evil doers, and the praife of them that do
well."—" I own them, in as far as they own Chriſt
and his cauſe," and ſuch like; yet both they, and their
accuſers, knew perfectly well, that theſe anſwers amounted to the fame thing, as a poſitive rejection of the
then prefent authority altogether; in as much as it was
well known to be the very reverfe of that, which they
deſcribed. Shall we ſtill be told, " It was not the CIVIL
AUTHORITY which the martyrs rejected and difowned ?"
If fo; the affertion muſt be applied to ſome other martyrs then theſe. That thoſe, who ſuffered, in the former period of that bloody perfecution, owned the authority in general, and fatisfied themfelves with openly
teſtifying againſt particular acts of mal-adminiſtration,
is well known; but no ſooner did the Explanatory Act
declare the fupremacy to be effential to the crown, than
the faithful in the land began to ſee the propriety of
wholly rejecting that authority, which was held and
exerciſed, on ſuch a footing. Many, indeed, faw it long
before. And though there be, among the fufferers, ſome
few inſtances of owning and praying for the king, even
after the year 1669, which is the date of the Explanatory Act; yet it was done in ſuch a conditional and qualified manner, as amounted to much the fame thing,
with a difavowal of his title to the throne of thefe covenanted kingdoms.

From the above extracts the following things are
fufficiently obvious. 1ſt. That all theſe martyrs in general, whoſe ſpeeches are recorded in the Cloud of
Witneſſes, and who ſuffered during the laſt eight years
of the perfecution, totally rejected the powers that then
were; both in their civil authority, and in their eccle-
fiaſtical fupremacy. The queſtion ordinarily put to them
was not, Own ye the king's fupremacy over the church?
but, Own ye the king's authority? To which they
anſwered in the negative. 2dly, That the openly avowed, and formal reafons of the rejection were, The ſinful
conditions, on which the authority was now held and
exerciſed; and not becauſe the rulers wanted the ma-

jority, of the nation upon their fide. The majority, both in church and ftate, thefe rulers unqueftionably had, for feveral years after the martyrs difowned their authority ; as every one, who attentively reads the hiftories of that period, will plainly fee. The Privy Councils, Parliaments, Armies, Civil and Military Courts of Judgment, together with the Judicatories of the Church, were all on the Ruler's fide ; while the martyrs were only a fmall defpifed handful of individual minifters and people. 3dly, That thefe noble fufferers, in the caufe of truth, were wholly unacquainted with the Seceding doctrine, " That all thofe who have a conftitution by the confent of civil fociety, are to be fubmitted unto for the Lord's fake, or, as having an inftitution from him." And, " That we are ordered to yield fubmiffion, without farther queftion, to every ordinance of man, every perfon in civil office by the will of fociety." † Thefe " chariots of Ifrael and the horfemen thereof" judged it requifite, to afk many farther queftions ; before they could, in confcience acknowledge and fubmit to the authority of thofe, who were then in civil office, by the will of even the national fociety. They muft find, if the ancient fundamental laws of the kingdom be overturned ; the Covenants, once folemnly fworn by all ranks in the land, broken and contemned ; the civil rights and liberties of the fubject deftroyed ; and the heritage of the Lord grievoufly oppreffed, by many wicked and Eraftian encroachments made upon it.— If they find thefe, and fuch like things now done, agreeably to the altered and new-modelled conftitution, and in virtue of a boafted prerogative royal ; this they reckon reafon, more than fufficient, for difowning the powers that be, even by the will of fociety. Which fentiments are juft the foul of Diffenting principles. 4thly, It is no lefs obvious from the above extracts, that Mr. Fletcher muft either retract thefe affertions, " It is falfe, that the martyrs difowned the civil authority of the Royal Brothers," and, " It was not the civil, but the ecclefiaftic ufurped authority, which they rejected ;" ‡

or

† See Declar. of Prin. p. 76, 77.   ‡ Def. p. 31, 32.

or, otherwife, he muft refufe the plain and honeft de-
clarations of thefe martyrs themfelves, as proper evidence in the cafe. He will alfo find himfelf reduced
to this other dilemma, either plainly, and honeftly, fpeak
it out; that thefe martyrs, whofe fpeeches are contained
in the Cloud of Witneffes, were wrong, and died in an
error, as we grant they were only fallible men; or elfe,
renounce that doctrine, that the minority have no right
to reject thefe powers, who are ftill acknowledged by
the body politic, or majority of the nation. Our opponent may take either of the fides he pleafes; but one
of them, nill he, will he, he muft take.

Mr. Fletcher, very unhappily, I fhould think, for his
own caufe, grants, " That it was the duty of the nation,
or of a majority in it, to reject and depofe their King
and inferior Rulers, becaufe they had turned the fceptre
of civil government into the ferpent of tyranny; and it
was their fin and punifhment that they bore the yoke of
oppreffion fo long." † To this we heartily fubfcribe;
and it exactly correfponds with the fentiments of thefe
fufferers themfelves, who, after the year 1669, were refifting unto blood, ftriving againft fin. In their caufes
for a public faft, they reckon their being fo far behind,
in this matter, as one of the fteps of defection, over
which they had to lament. Now, to have rejected and
depofed the King, and inferior rulers, would certainly
have been to difown them, with a witnefs, both in civil
and ecclefiaftic things. It is therefore granted, that it
was the duty of the nation, totally to reject the authority of Charles II. and James VII. not only at the time
when the martyrs did it, but even long before; for " It
was their fin that they bore the yoke of oppreffion fo
long." Let it alfo be obferved, that if the faid authority, as is agreed on both fides, fhould have been rejected, even to the depofition of the powers which then
were; it muft have been unlawful authority; for
Mr. Fletcher well knows that " Difloyalty," and certainly rejection and depofition are nothing lefs, " to the

JUST

† Def. p. 35.

JUST and LEGAL authority of princes, is rebellion againſt God, and very hurtful to the religion of Jeſus Chriſt."† Query, How doth it appear, that the authority of Charles II. and James VII. who "turned the ſceptre of civil government into the ſerpent of tyranny," was unlawful authority, which, Mr. Fletcher himſelf being judge, ſhould have been totally diſowned and rejeſted by the whole nation, who ſhould have depoſed theſe princes; while, at the ſame time, the authority of a Pharaoh, a Nebuchadnezzar, or a monſtrous Nero, who, at leaſt in an equal, or rather ſtill more terrible manner, turned the ſceptre of civil government, into the ſerpent of tyranny," was the lawful authority ordained of God, to which the Lord's people were to be ſubjeſt, not only for wrath, but for conſcience' ſake. How comes it to paſs, that among powers of the ſame kind, and anſwering to the ſame deſcription, ſome are lawful, and muſt not be reſiſted, but under pain of damnation; while others are unlawful, and ſhould be rejeſted and depoſed? A proper ſolution will be very acceptable to Diſſenters, and to ſome others too. It will not, I hope, be pled, that the mere ſinfully delaying to perform a plain duty, could alter the nature of things, and legitimate a government, which was, in itſelf, poſitively ſinful, and tyrannical. Nor will the diſtinguiſhing between the majority and the minority, be any ſalvo in the matter. It hath been fairly granted, that it was the ſin of the majority, to own and ſubmit to theſe tyrannical powers, ſo long as they did; for, inſtead of that, they ſhould have depoſed them. What was the ſin of the majority, could not, ſurely, be the duty of the minority; unleſs that either ſin and duty be convertible terms, or that the mere will of a majority be the ſtandard of right and wrong, independent of JEHOVAH's will. We are therefore neceſſarily brought to this concluſion, That there have been, and ſtill may be caſes, in which even the powers that aſtually exiſt, in the courſe of adorable providence, and by the will of a nation too, ought not

to

† Scrip. Loy. p. 48.

to be owned, neither by the majority, nor minority. And though the one should, for a time, either not discern their duty, or neglect to perform it; that can be no proper reason why the other should do so likewife. So soon as the way of truth is discovered, whether by more or fewer; it ought to be actually followed.

Mr. Fletcher next proceeds to oppose, what he seems to reckon his opponent's doctrine, concerning prayer for wicked Magistrates. † I am truly forry to find, that this part of the dispute also is managed in a very uncandid manner. I should think, it is scarcely possible, that Mr. Fletcher, if he read without prejudice, could really persuade himself to believe, that ever Mr. Steven, in his Letter, taught any such doctrine, as that which he here sets himself to oppose. Mr. Steven freely grants, that we should pray for all forts of men in general, civil rulers by no means excepted; but the praying of which he is speaking, and of which alone he complains, is a praying for tyrants, or for any unlawful rulers whatsoever, in that formal, prescribed, and unqualified manner, which is considered, on all hands, as importing a recognizing of their title; while, at the fame time, the person so praying cannot, in judgment and conscience, approve of the fundamental laws and conditions, on the footing of which these rulers hold and exercise their power. ‡ This, and this alone, is the fort of prayer, which Mr. Steven opposes. But the judicious and candid reader will eafily perceive, that every sentence of what Mr. Fletcher here says on the subject, strikes directly against a fictitious doctrine of his own contrivance, and which was never taught by any Diffenter, in Scotland; namely, that we should not pray for Magistrates at all, even when clothed with lawful authority; and, especially, that we should not pray for wicked rulers, nor indeed for wicked men of any description, who are our avowed enemies, neither in one shape nor other, no not for conviction, repentance, or reformation unto them; but should rather wish
the

† Def. p. 36,—50.   ‡ See his Let. p. 14,—26.

L

the vengeance of the Almighty to be inflicted upon
them. This, and this alone, is the doctrine which
Mr. Fletcher oppofes. And it was, certainly, as ftrongly
oppofed by Mr. Steven, both in principle and practice,
and is ftill as ftrongly oppofed, by all his furviving
brethren, to a man, as ever it could be by Seceders,
or any other. Let any fenfible and impartial judge,
carefully compare together thefe parts of the Letter
and Defence, cited at the bottom of the page ; and it
fhall be freely fubmitted to him, whether the obfervations now made, be juft; and, confequently, whether
the whole of Mr. Steven's reafoning, on this part of
the fubject, do not ftand exactly as it was, without
being ever fo much as touched by the Defence. Our
opponent's mode of thus, fuddenly and unexpectedly,
fhifting ground, and totally altering the ftate of the
queftion, in the courfe of his replies, † is exceedingly
unfair. It may, perhaps, impofe upon the weak, fuper-
ficial and inattentive reader ; but the deceit muft be
feen at once, by every man of penetration, who carefully looks into the fubject. I hope we agree, that
it is duty to pray for all forts of men in general, whether they be kings, or fubjects; high, or low; rich, or
poor ; profeffors, or profane ; friends, or foes. The
Scripture makes only one exception, in the cafe of
perfons known to have finned the fin unto death ; or,
which amounts to the fame thing, known, by a particular revelation of the divine mind, to be already doom-
ed unto everlafting deftruction. And we muft all be
guided by the Holy Scriptures, with regard to the extent of our prayers. The difpute is about the particular modes of praying; what fuch and fuch forts of
prayer neceffarily imply.

In the 20th. page of his Letter, Mr. Steven had faid,
" The Church and her members have often prayed, that
kings might be nurfing fathers, and their queens her
nurfing mothers, and judges might be reftored as at the
firft, and counfellors as at the beginning, that officers
might

† See Def. p. 39.

might be peace, and exactors righteousness, when such
had no real being, as to them, but in the promise; and
yet were not branded and abused, for praying for magistracy, or lawful authority, in the abstract." Does
Mr. Fletcher venture to deny this? No; neither he, nor
any man alive, can deny it, but at the expence of contradicting the Sacred Oracles. The prophecy, referred
to, * not only looks forward to the return of the Jews
from Babylon, though even that was then a future bleffing, but it evidently looks forward to the calling of the
Gentiles, in New Testament times; an event which was
not to take place, till several hundred years after the
prophecy was uttered. But it was certainly the duty,
and would be the actual exercise of faithful wrestlers,
who waited for the consolation of Israel, to plead the
accomplishment of what the Lord had graciously spoken;
while as yet they saw it only afar off. It is observable,
that in both the passages, to which Mr. Steven's asser-
tion alludes, the calling of the Gentiles is expressly mentioned, in the verse immediately preceding. However,
although Mr. Fletcher can neither contradict his opponent's doctrine, nor offer so much as the shadow of a
reason, to shew that it is false; yet something must be
said, in return. He tells us, that what Mr. Steven said,
—" Is very weak and trifling reasoning to one who
knows, that their is neither precept nor example in the
Book of God to warrant a *praying for, and a wishing-
well to the ordinance of Magistracy in the abstract.*—
Which," says he, " is a non-entity, and absolutely in-
capable of receiving any benefit, by prayer and good
wishes." † Is Mr. Steven speaking here of magistracy
in the abstract, when he mentions, in express terms,
" kings, queens, judges, counsellors, officers and exactors?" But if, after all, magistracy in the abstract be,
indeed, a non-entity; it is great pity, that Mr. Fletcher
should have opened so many powerful batteries, for its
destruction. And it is no less pity, that he should have
inadvertently stammered on that mode of expression,
which

---

* Isa. xlix. 23. and lx. 17.   † Def. p. 38.

which we find in the 55th. page of the Loyalist:
" Magistracy is an ordinance instituted by God."
To be confistent, he should certainly have said, Magistrates, in the concrete; for to say, that a non-entity
is instituted by God, would be intolerable. Mr. Fletcher
proceeds, and tells us, " When prayer is made by
the Church, that Kings may be nursing-fathers, &c.
it may be, and very frequently is understood of civil
rulers presently exisling." * Be it so; that makes
nothing against Mr. Steven's doctrine: for we have just
shewn, that it also has been, and yet may be understood
of civil rulers, who have, for the present, no exisfence,
except in the promise; and who may not be actually
obtained, for hundreds of years after the promise is
given. Which is all that is necessary, for establishing
our doctrine. But, " It is the duty of Protesfants in
Popish countries, to pray, that their Popish Magisfrates
may become nursing-fathers to the church." † Before
they could properly become nursing-fathers to a Pro-
testant, or Prefbyterian Church ; it would, I apprehend,
be requisite to have as great an alteration made, with
respect both to the footing on which they hold their authority, and to their external profession of religion, as
that which Dissenters themselves wish, with respect to
the Britifh rulers, and their constitution. We are further told, " To plead, that we should pray for Magisfrates when they are good, and for Magisfracy in the
abstract when they are bad, is to make the changeable
difpensations of providence the rule of duty." ‡ But
neither Mr. Steven, nor any of his brethren, ever
taught any such doctrine. They teach, that when magisfrates, who have a just and legal title to the places
which they fill, are actually obtained by a people ; it is,
then, the duty of that people, to pray for these magisfrates, formally considered as such ; sincerely wishing,
that the Lord may gracioufly bless, direct and prosper
them, in the administration of their righteous government. But when, in the righteous judgment of God,
vile

* Def. p. 38. † p. 38, 39. ‡ p. 39.

vile men, who act the tyrant, and ufurp a blafphemous
fupremacy over the church of Chrift, happen to be ex-
alted; then, and in all fuch cafes, we have no warrant from
Scripture to pray for fuch monfters, formally confidered
as rulers; becaufe they either never had any juft title
to that dignity; or, if they ever had, they have now
wholly forfeited it, by violating the fundamental conditions of government. Yet for thefe very perfons, fimply confidered as fellow-men and finners of the human
race, or, if you will, as unjuft rulers fet up by the nation, but evidently holding and exercifing their power
on finful terms, we may earneftly implore the pardoning
mercy and rich grace of God; wifhing that they may
be brought to fincere repentance, an open renouncing
of the finful conditions, on which they have been advanced, and to a fpeedy amendment. This was exactly
the cafe with the martyrs, efpecially during the laft eight
years of the perfecution. They pofitively refufed to
pray, in the loofe, unqualified and prefcribed form,
" God fave the King;" becaufe that was confidered by
both them and their perfecutors, as recognizing his title
to the magiftratical power; the juftnefs of which they
could by no means grant. But does this fay, that they
indulged malice in their heart, or had any perfonal hatred at the men, who were then in power, by the will
of fociety; or, that they had any objection to pray for
their bodily health, temporal happinefs, or everlafting
falvation? Certainly not: he who would charge them
with this, would, indeed, bring a " falfe accufation.
againft men, of whom the world was not worthy;
would reprefent them not as martyrs for the caufe of
God and truth, but as evil doers, as rebels againft the
authority of Chrift."

I am aware, that our opponent will immediately cry
out, We have compared the Britifh Rulers to monfters,
tyrants and ufurpers; and at the expence of doing fo,
have defended our refufal to pray for them, in the ufual
form. No fuch thing, however, is intended. Diffenters can eftablifh every iota of their doctrine, without
ever confidering thefe Rulers either as monfters, tyrants,

or

or ufurpers. They know, as well as Seceders, that the Britifh Magiftrates rule on the footing of the Conftitution, framed, and, from time to time, varioufly modified, by the reprefentatives of the nation. Yea, they rule by the confent of the majority in the kingdom. But the fame general principle may be gone upon, while the feveral objeēts, to which it is applied, are much diverfified. We may refufe to recognize the title of fome rulers, becaufe they are monfters and tyrants; and refufe to recognize the title of others, becaufe, however amiable their perfonal charaēter, or mild their adminiftration, yet the fundamental conditions of their advancement are pofitively finful. It is the prayer, neceffarily involving an approbation of fuch conditions, againft which we contend. The fum of what Diffenters teach, on the fubjeēt, is plainly and fimply this, Unlefs they can be fatisfied, in their own mind, with refpeēt to the magiftrate's juft and Scriptural title unto the place which he aētually fills; they have no clearnefs to pray, in fuch an unqualified form, as is confidered, both by themfelves and the requirers, to be a recognizing of that title : meanwhile, they can fincerely wifh the perfons well, in body and foul, in time and through eternity. If Mr. Fletcher can prove this to be abfurd and erroneous; we are willing to hear him. But he muft go to work in fome other manner than by continually manufaēturing doētrines, which we never taught, and of which we never entertained the moft diftant thought.

To what he reckons his opponent's mode of praying, Mr. Fletcher alfo objeēts, that " It makes the changeable difpenfations of providence the rule of duty." But we fhould have expeēted him to have been the laft man, who would have objeēted to this, even fuppofing, though it is not really the cafe, that Mr. Steven had faid it. Mr. Fletcher and his brethren have uniformly taught, That all providential magiftrates, are alfo preceptive; i. e. if language have any meaning at all, Whoever, in courfe of holy providence, aētually fills a throne, by the voice of a majority in the nation, let him be otherwife what he may, he is a lawful magiftrate; it is

agree-

agreeable to the precept, that he fhould reign; and he hath a juft claim to confcientious obedience, from every foul within the territory. But it has often happened, that the fame perfon has been a fubject to day, murdered his prince, and afcended his throne to morrow, yea and been acknowledged, or allowed to reign, by the people too. † We will alfo find, in the courfe of divine providence, a rebellious Abfalom poffeffing the royal refidence and attended by the majority of Ifrael to day, but put to death; and David, his father, reigning tomorrow. According to Seceding doctrine; thefe ftriking difpenfations of providence would have taught, before the rebellion to have prayed, God fave King David; when Abfalom was at the height of his career, God fave King Abfalom; and again, when he was dead, and his father re-afcended the throne, God fave King David. Of fuch doctrine it would appear to be a pretty native confequence, That the changeable difpenfations of providence are, in fome things at leaft, the rule of duty. No perfon, who reads, with candour, the Sacred Hiftory of Abfalom's rebellion, can hefitate a moment about his having the majority on his fide. It is not indeed faid in fo, many words; but feveral parts of the narrative are remarkably expreffive. He ufed his infinuating methods with " All Ifrael that came to the king for judgment. So Abfalom ftole the hearts of the men of Ifrael." He " fent fpies throughout all the tribes of Ifrael.—The confpiracy was ftrong; for the people increafed continually with Abfalom. There came a meffenger to David, faying, The hearts of the men of Ifrael are after Abfalom." The counfel which advifed, " That all Ifrael fhould be gathered unto him, from Dan even to Beer-fheba, as the fand that is by the fea for multitude, and that he fhould go to battle in his own perfon," was that which was approved and adopted by " Abfalom and all the men of Ifrael." · It is alfo faid, " The people of Ifrael were flain before the fervants of David; and there was there a great flaughter that day, of twenty thouf-

† See, befides human hiftory, 2 Kings xv.

thoufand men." *i. e.* Twenty thoufand of the rebels, as it is generally underftood. Yet even that vaft number doth not feem to have been much miffed from the general multitude, who had anointed Abfalom over them; and who returned again to their allegiance unto their lawful prince. — " All the people were at ftrife, throughout all the tribes of Ifrael, faying, The king faved us out of the hands of our enemies.—And Abfalom, whom we anointed over us, is dead in battle." The terms are ftill remarkably general and comprehenfive. But the royal army is donominated thus, " The fervants of David." A term more particular and reftrictive-like. *

Mr. Fletcher is exceedingly difpleafed with his opponent's expofition of Jer. xxix. 7. Mr. Steven, in his Letter had faid, " It is manifeft, that this prayer recommended to the captives, includes no duty they owed, either to the Babylonifh Monarch, or to the city and the inhabitants thereof, as if either had been a bleffing unto them. On the contrary, they were a curfe, and the rod of God's judgment to punifh them for their fins, for the removal of which, in his own time, it was their duty to pray. The fubject matter of the prayer, therefore, is folely their own peace and happinefs, during the time appointed them to fojourn there." † After carefully reading the facred account of the whole matter, one would think that even prejudice itfelf could fcarcely find an objection to this interpretation. Yet, fays Mr. Fletcher, " Every man, poffeffed of common fenfe, muft fee, that this comment is a bare-faced falfehood. The peace of the city is manifeftly the fubject matter of this prayer : ' Seek the peace of the city, and pray ' unto God for it.'— Whether it be right in the fight of God, to hearken unto Mr. Steven more than unto God, let the reader judge." ‡ But a little more patience, if you pleafe. So far is it from being any contradiction, for one to fay, " The peace of the city was the fubject-matter of the prayer;" and another to fay, " Their own

own peace, while fojourning in the city, was folely the fubject-matter of the prayer," that the two affertions are perfectly confiflent; yea, the one neceffarily involves the other. Their own peace, and the peace of the city, at that time, and in their peculiar circumftances, were fynonimous terms. Hence the Spirit of God exprefsly affigns it as the formal reafon, why they fhould pray for the peace of the city, becaufe in the peace thereof they themfelves were to have peace. Mr. Steven fpeaks not a word againft praying for the peace of the city; but he teaches, that the command, to do fo, was not given, on account of any duty of that kind, which the captives owed to the Babylonifh Monarch, or the inhabitants of the city, confidered as the rod of God's judgment to punifh them for their fins; the alone view of it, in which the prayer can make any thing for Mr. Fletcher's purpofe; but it was given, becaufe their own peace was neceffarily involved in the peace of the city. Hence a proper concern for the prefervation of the church, while appearing like a bufh in the midft of the flames, loudly called for this feafonable exercife.

At the foot of the fame page, it is fuppofed, that Mr. Steven contradicts himfelf; becaufe, after refufing, as is alledged, that the peace of the city was the fubject-matter of the prayer, he, in the very next fentence fays, that " the command to the captives was merely pofitive and temporary, during their feventy years refidence in that place; at the expiration of which, their prayer was entirely reverfed." Says Mr. Fletcher, " He cannot mean, that the prayer for their own peace was reverfed, and therefore muft mean their prayer for the peace of the city." The unbiaffed reader, however, will eafily difcern, that there is not the leaft fhadow of contradiction in Mr. Steven's doctrine. During the feventy years captivity, the peace of the city Babylon, and the peace of the Jews, who dwelt in it, were infeparably connected together; fo that praying for the one, was, as hath juft been faid, praying for the other alfo. When that difmal period expired, and the Lord's people were brought from the place of their long captivity; the connection

M   was

was totally diffolved. Perfecuting Babylon now appeared by herfelf, as having filled up the meafure of her iniquity; as drunk with the blood of the faints; and as juft about to receive blood to drink, from the hand of an avenging God. Now the captives were to reverfe, not indeed the prayer for their own peace, but the temporary manner of praying for that, by feeking the peace of Babylon; which once neceffarily involved the other in it, but did fo no longer. It was uniformly their duty, before the captivity, during its continuance, and ever after, to feek their own peace, as the church of the living God; yea, and alfo to pray for repentance and reformation to all forts of men, even the moft atrocioufly wicked and perfecuting enemies not excepted; fo long as the Lord himfelf had not pofitively declared their final doom, by fome direct and explicit revelation from heaven. But even this doth not fay, that ever the peace of Babylon, either during the captivity, or afterwards, was fought properly on her own account, confidered as the open enemy of God and religion; as holding this malicious language, concerning Jerufalem, "Raze, raze it to the foundation;" and as now folemnly devoted to deftruction, by the Righteous Judge of all the earth; yea, and the awful defigns of Heaven, with regard to her final ruin, already clearly made known to the church. That there may be peculiar circumftances, in which it would be improper to feek the peace of a city, or people, the God of truth himfelf plainly fignifies; when, fpeaking of the polluted land and its inhabitants, he thus enjoins his ancient Ifrael, " Give not your daughters unto their fons, neither take their daughters unto your fons, nor feek their peace or their wealth for ever." † Babylon-like, they were devoted to deftruction.

The ftriking refemblance between Old, and New Teftament Babylon, deferves our fpecial notice here. What Myftery Babylon the Great, the mother of harlots and abominations of the earth, is to the New Teftament Church;

† Ezra ix. 12. comp. Deut. xxiii. 6.

Church; the fame, fubftantially, was ancient, perfecuting
Babylon to the Old Teftament Church; as every one,
willing to be inftructed from the Book of God, may
clearly fee, by comparing the xiii. and xiv. chapters
of Ifaiah, and the l. and li. of Jeremiah, with the ii.
of the 2d. Epiftle to the Theffalonians, and the xvii.
xviii. and part of the xix. of the Revelation.——
The great characteriftics of pride, haughtinefs, felf-
fufficiency, and arrogantly affuming Jehovah's prerogatives, are equally applied, in both cafes. The fame
blood-thirfty and perfecuting difpofition, in attempting
to wear out the faints of the Moft High, is afcribed to
the one, and to the other. The very awful and alarm-
ing judgments of Heaven are denounced againft both,
in language remarkably fimilar. While their final ruin
refpectively, is, with like clearnefs, revealed to the
church; as affording her a fong of everlafting triumph.
But, concerning the man of fin, or the Antichrift, in
New Teftament times, Mr. Fletcher fays, " Some Seceders are not fond of praying for this notable blafphemer,
becaufe Paul calls him, *The Son of perdition.*" † If you,
Sir, mean to rank amongft thefe Seceders; pray, where
is your confiftency, in fo ftrenuoufly defending prayer
for the peace and profperity of Old Teftament Antichrift,
or bloody Babylon, pofitively declared by the Lord himfelf to be near unto deftruction; while you fcruple to
pray for the peace of New Teftament Antichrift, though
in the very fame predicament? A proper folution will
be very acceptable. For my own part, I fhould think,
that the true church of God might have been very eafily
excufed, in earneftly praying for the deftruction of the
one, as well as of the other. Nor does it feem to be
any thing more than a praying, agreeably to the Third
Petition, "Thy will be done on earth, as it is in heaven."
And in unifon with the cry of the fouls under the altar,
" How long, O Lord, holy and true, doft thou not judge
and avenge our blood on them that dwell on the earth?" ‡
There is nothing, therefore, in the reverfed prayer,
" enough

"enough to make both the ears to tingle;" as Mr. Fletcher, groundlefsly, fuppofes. Neither has he any proper reafon to fay, that " Mr. Steven mentions the following texts, Jer. li. 35. and Pfal. cxxxvii. 8, 9. to prove the Anti-chriſtian doctrine of praying for curſes to our enemies." †
He mentions them, Sir, to prove, that after the church hath her Lord's will clearly made known to her, ſhe is warranted to pray for the deſtruction of Antichriſt, and his doctrines both. He never drops the moſt diſtant hint about praying for curſes to our enemies in general; concerning whoſe final perdition we have no particular revelation from the Lord. But thoſe, concerning whom he fays, that the captives, inſtead of praying any longer for their peace, were now to pray for the vengeance of the Almighty to be inflicted on them, were plainly and pofitively declared, by the Spirit of truth, to be appointed for deſtruction. Befides, as Mr. Steven, when ſhewing that the prayer was to be reverſed, expreſſes himſelf, in the very words of the texts adduced; it is impoſſible to controvert his doctrine, without controverting theſe texts likewiſe.

To weaken the force of Mr. Steven's argument, his opponent fuppofes, " Either he never knew, or has forgotten, that the vengeance of the Almighty was in-flicted on Bablon, before the return of the captivity." ‡ In proof of which pofition both profane and facred hif-tory are produced. That the terrible devaſtations and ravages of war were experienced in Babylon, at the time, and by the inſtruments alluded to, and that the kingdom was divided and given to the Medes and Per-fians, before the Lord turned the captivity of his people, are truths, which, I fuppofe, were as well known to Mr. Steven, as they are to Mr Fletcher. But that theſe beginnings of ſorrows ſhould be any contradiction to their drinking the more full cup of indignation, a long time after, is what will not, perhaps, be ſo eaſily diſcer-ned. Mr. Fletcher himſelf will, probably find it too hard a taſk to prove, either from facred or profane hiftory,

† Def. p. 43.   ‡ p. 44.

tory, that previous to the return of the captivity,
" Babylon became heaps, a dwelling-place for dragons,
an aſtoniſhment and an hiſſing without inhabitant," in
accompliſhment of God's threatened vengeance againſt
her.   Let the Oracles of Truth decide the controverſy:
" And it ſhall come to paſs, WHEN SEVENTY YEARS ARE
ACCOMPLISHED that I will puniſh the king of Babylon,
and that nation, ſaith the Lord, for their iniquity, and
the land of the Caldeans, and will make it perpetual
deſolations." *   It is worthy of notice, that the terrible
deſolating judgments, to be inflicted upon Babylon, are
threatened in the very next verſes to that which contains the reverſed prayer, of which Mr. Steven ſpeaks,
and which was to be the church's amen, to the righteous vengeance of JEHOVAH's temple. †   There is not,
therefore, ſo much as the ſhadow of a reaſon, for charg-
ing him with " either never knowing, or having forgotten, that the vengeance was inflicted already."   It
was ſo only in part; but not to the extent either of the
threatening, or of the prayer for its accompliſhment.

But theſe paſſages, Jer. li. 35. and Pſal. cxxxvii. 8, 9.
ſays Mr. Fletcher, " are ſo far from proving the doctrine
of this reverſed prayer, that they prove it to be a mere
fiction, vanity and a lie." ‡   What he intends by this,
it is not eaſy to ſay.   That the ſenſe which he impoſes
on Mr. Steven's doctrine about reverſing the prayer,
turns out a mere fiction, is what, I apprehend, every
judicious and candid reader will ſee, at the firſt glance
of the two pamphlets.   But does he mean to deny the
poſitive and ſtubborn fact?   Mr. Steven had ſaid, " That
at the experation of the ſeventy years' captivity, the
prayer for the peace of the city was entirely reverſed."
The Sacred Oracles, which he immediately produced,
in proof of the aſſertion, ſay expreſsly ſo too: " The
violence done to me, and to my fleſh, be upon Babylon,
ſhall the inhabitant of Zion ſay."   Is this ſtill to pray
for the peace of the city Babylon!   Muſt Scripture-teſti-
mony

---

* Jer. xxv. 12. See alſo Brown's Dict. on the word BABYLON.

† See Jer. li. 35,—37.   ‡ Def. p. 45.

timony alfo be rejeƈted; merely becaufe it is adduced by
Mr. Steven! " Let it be obferved," fays Mr. Fletcher,
" that the paffages quoted by Mr. Steven, and others of
a fimilar nature, are to be confidered rather as prediƈtions,
than as prayers." * Be it fo: what is the confequence?
If once the Lord be pleafed to foretel what he intends
to do with fuch and fuch avowed, perfecuting, and irreconcileable enemies of his church; what can be the great
harm in praying, Thy will be done; or in wifhing that the
prediƈtion may be fulfilled? Befides, it is to be feared,
that Mr. Fletcher's objeƈtion to his opponent's doƈtrine,
will here meet himfelf very full in the face. " Did
Mr. Fletcher never know, or has he forgotten, that the
vengeance here foretold was inflicted on Babylon, before
the captivity; and therefore could never be the fubjeƈt
matter of a prophecy?" To prediƈt or foretel what has
already happened, feems to be little lefs abfurd, than to
pray for it. While unreafonably anxious to condemn
others; we are in danger of alfo fometimes condemning
ourfelves.

The precepts, prayers of the faints, example of the
Great King of faints, and the doƈtrine of the Larger
Catechifm, all produced in the following pages of the
Defence, † are certainly good and worthy of our ferious
attention. But it would be very unreafonable to fuppofe either Mr. Fletcher, or indeed any reader of an
ordinary capacity, fo very ignorant as to believe, that
they militate any thing againft the doƈtrine contained
in the Letter from Crookedholm. The moft of them
have no refpeƈt at all to praying for magiftrates as fuch,
either of one defcription or another. Such of them as
look that way, recommend no fuch thing as praying for
wicked, or unlawful magiftrates, in that general and
unqualified form, which plainly recognizes their title;
though that is evidently the matter in difpute.

In the remaining part of this feƈtion, ‡ Mr. Fletcher
feems to glory over his opponent, now profelyted, as he
fuppofes, to his own doƈtrine, and fo come over to the
camp of the Loyalift. Mr. Steven had made fome conceffions,

---

* Def. p. 45.   † p. 46,—50.   ‡ p. 50,—59.

ceffions, with refpect to paffive fubjection, in cafes of neceffity: * Mr Fletcher replies, " Pray, Sir, how comes it to pafs, that the fame truth from the mouth of the Loyalift, rows into the deep fea of tyranny ; but in your mouth, it looks unto the lofty mountains and little hills, that bring peace unto the people by righteoufnefs?. The folution of the difficulty in your next will be very obliging." † It hath pleafed the Great Lord of life and death, who affures us, " Our days are determined, the number of our months is with him, and he hath fet our bounds that we cannot pafs," to call the much refpected Author of the Letter from this fcene of mortality into the world of fpirits. Speaking after the manner of men ; by his death, the church militant undoubtedly fuftains a great lofs ; and the caufe, defended in the Letter, wants an able advocate. Had it been the will of providence, to have fpared him, until he fhould have accomplifhed his defign of replying to Mr. Fletcher's Defence ; he would certainly have found no difficulty, in folving the queftion before us. Even the weakeft of his furviving brethren may find it a very eafy matter.

If Mr. Fletcher, in producing the above examples, ‡ be pleading for no other fort of fubjection to the prefent Britifh Magiftrates, than that which thefe examples recommend ; Diffenters can very readily, in full confiftency with their avowed principles, fubfcribe the doctrine. If he only mean that paffive fubmiffion, particularly fpecified in fo many words by Mr. Steven in all his conceffions ; wifhing us, in the prefent cafe, patiently to bear fuch injuries as we cannot poffibly avoid, till the Lord in his mercy may be pleafed to grant us deliverance ; to conduct ourfelves peaceably ; and to fubmit to all fuch things as are in their own nature innocent and lawful, but at the fame time have no connection with recognizing the authority ; to all this, fo far as I know, Diffenters never had any objections ; and all this they can eafily grant, without ever fhifting the ground, on which they have all along ftood, and without

out approaching one fingle ftep towards the camp of the Loyalift. The purpofe for which the Loyalift produceth thefe examples, is, if he fpeak to the point at all, to prove the lawfulnefs of the prefent Government, even all circumftances confidered, as the authority ordained of God; to which we owe fubjection, not only for wrath, but for confcience' fake. If he mean the examples to eftablifh this; neither Mr. Steven, nor any other Diffenter who ever wrote on the fubject, hath, as yet, granted that they do. If he do not mean, that they are any proof of this; all his labour on the fubject, from firft to laft, hath been totally in vain. The grand queftion, about owning, or difowning, in the proper fenfe of the term, ftill remains untouched. After all that hath been faid, in both the editions of the Loyalift, and in the Defence; we have only afcertained, what was never denied, namely, that feeing it was the duty of the Lord's people, when they could not help their fituation, to yield paffive fubjection, and peaceably comply, in fuch things as are in themfelves innocent and lawful, even under the moft tyrannical and perfecuting rulers, in whofe dominions providence ordered their lot; much more is it their duty to yield the fame fort of fubjection, and comply in fimilar things, under milder rulers, whether their title, when all circumftances are confidered, be lawful or unlawful. This is evidently the amount of the whole. And we may furely regret, that fo much pains fhould have been taken, to perfuade us of the fun's being up at noon-day.

ANIMADVERSIONS ON SECTION IV.

The detection, of what Mr. Fletcher is pleafed to call, " Mifreprefentations, Calumnies and Contradictions," is the declared defign of this part of the Defence. It is prefumed, however, that the candid reader, upon ferious examination, will find. that thefe terms are very ill applied. Let us fee what thefe fuppofed mifreprefentations are.

Mr.

Mr. Fletcher firſt complains, that his opponent, in almoſt every page of his Letter, repreſents the Loyaliſt as teaching, "That mankind ſhould bear the yoke of ſlavery, even when it is in the power of their hand to throw it off." * A charge which he poſitively refuſes. Mr. Steven indeed affirms, "That the argument from Scripture precepts and examples, AS STATED AND APPLIED BY Mr. FLETCHER, proves that men, eſpecially the ſaints, muſt be ſubject to the yoke of oppreſſion, whether they have power to throw it off or not." † And he had ſufficient reaſon to ſay ſo. While condeſcending on ſeveral higher powers, to whom the Lord's people were ſubject, Mr. Fletcher mentions among others, "The tyrants of Egypt, of Babylon, and Rome." And then ſubjoins, "—If it was the duty of the people of God, in all paſt generations, to obey the juſt authority of the moſt froward princes, &c. ‡ Our opponent being his own interpreter, amongſt the froward princes, whoſe juſt authority we ſhould obey, tyrants have a place. But he adds, that this was to be done by the Lord's people, "When it was not in their power to break the rod of their oppreſſors." Be it ſo ; he alſo, elſewhere, declares, "To pray for a bleſſing to civil rulers, and for long life and proſperity, not only to the MEEK AND GENTLE, but alſo to the FROWARD, is warranted by Scripture precept and example." ┼ "The juſt authority of tyrants," for they are ranked among the froward princes, appears to me rather a ſoleciſm. But be that as it may : if to obey, as juſt and lawful, the authority of froward princes, ſuch as, "the tyrants of Egypt, of Babylon, and Rome," and "to pray for a bleſſing, for long life and proſperity unto them," in their official capacity, be conſiſtent with throwing off the yoke of their government, even though it were in our power ; I confeſs, I cannot ſee it. He who refiſteth the power, to whom ſuch duties are owing, refiſteth the ordinance of God ; the inſpired Oracles being judge. But, according

* Def. p. 60. † Let. p. 128. ‡ Def. p. 50, 51.
┼ Scrip. Loy. p. 29.

ing to the exprefs doctrine of the Loyalift, thefe duties
are owing to all froward princes in general, "the tyrants of Egypt, of Babylon, and Rome," not excepted;
therefore, he who refifteth, or cafteth off, the yoke of
thefe froward princes, or tyrants, refifteth the ordinance
of God. Can we both fubmit to their authority
as juft, praying for a blessing upon them in the
exercife of it; and caft it off, at the fame time?
If Mr. Fletcher reply; it is hoped, that he will not
put us off with fome general bold affertion; but that
he will plainly inform his reader, whether or not it be
truly the doctrine of the Loyalift, and Defence, "that
we fhould fubmit to the juft authority, and pray for a
blessing upon the government of froward princes, even
fuch as the tyrants of Egypt, of Babylon, and Rome."
And then, Whether it be not a native confequence, that
we cannot confiftently both do that, and caft off their
authority, even though it were in our power.

A fecond mifreprefentation is faid to be, Blaming the
Loyalift for "comprehending the meek and gentle, and
the froward prince, within the precept and example."
"To this Mr. Fletcher replies, "It is not I, Sir, but
an infpired Apoftle."—And for proof cites 1 Pet. ii. 18. †
The Apoftle, in that paffage, is evidently cautioning
againft, either the abfurd doctrine of fome Judaizing
zealots, who foolifhly imagined, that it was inconfiftent with the natural rights of mankind, to be fervant
to any man upon earth; or the no lefs abfurd notion
of thofe, who falfely fuppofed, that the Chriftian religion
diffolved the bonds of human fociety, and deftroyed the
diftinction of fuperiors and inferiors, efpecially when
the one party was Infidel, and the other Chriftian. To
guard againft fuch miftakes, the Apoftle teaches, that
Chriftianity does not diffolve the relation, already fixed;
between mafter and fervant. As though he had faid,
Even fuch of you as are flaves, or bond fervants, and
fo have it not in your power to throw off your infidel
mafters' yoke, after you yourfelves have embraced
Chriftianity, ought ftill to behave in a patient,

peace-

† Def. p. 61.

peaceable and fubmiffive manner, towards your fuperiors. Yea, though they fhould frown upon you,
and ufe you even more roughly, on account of your religion; yet endeavour, through grace, to fuffer patiently.
Let not your good be evil fpoken of, by giving them
irritating and, provoking language, or rifing up in a
riotous manner againft them ; but rather pour out your
complaint unto God, who hears the fighs of the pri-
foners. Let the fame be the fludy of thofe voluntary
fervants, who, previous to their embracing Chriftianity,
had agreed with their infidel mafters, to ferve them for
a certain length of time, upon condition of receiving
certain wages, ftipulated in the paction. Behave yourfelves inoffenfively and fubmiffively, till your term be
expired; and then you will be free to make a better
choice. Thus fhall you, by well-doing, put to filence
the ignorance of foolifh men ; and wipe off the reproach,
unjuftly caft upon the Chriftian religion. Such feems
to be the Apoftle's fcope. But what connection all this
hath with praying for a bleffing, for long life and profperity, to tyrants and ufurpers, for in the clafs of froward rulers thefe are allowed to be comprehended, it is,
I confefs, not eafy to fee. Becaufe fervants, whether
brought into this fituation by neceffity, or by paction,
fhould, during the appointed time of their fervitude,
peaceably do their work, and endeavour, with as much
patience as poffible, to bear even the frowns and mal-
treatment of fuch mafters as are furly and froward in
their difpofition; how it will neceffarily follow, that we
fhould pray for a bleffing to froward princes, or tyrants,
in fuch form as to recognize their authority, would
require to be fhewn in fome other manner, than by bare
affertion. It is the comprehending alike, both the lawful civil ruler, and the froward prince or tyrant, within
thefe precepts and examples, which recommend prayer
of this kind, concerning which Mr. Steven complains
upon the Loyalift : as any one may fee, by looking into
his Letter. Mr. Steven very juftly confiders praying,
in a general and unqualified manner, for a bleffing on
their perfon and government, and for long life and pro-

fperity

fperity to them, in their official capacity, as an owning
of their authority. But having found the Loyalift
obliged to confefs, that lawful authority and tyranny
are fpecifically different; he might furely, with full
confiflency, afterwards blame him, for putting thefe two
on the fame level, in the prayers for which he pleads. *
" There were," fays Mr. Fletcher, " faints in Cefar's
houfehold, and this precept, no doubt, bound them to
be fubject to their royal mafter in the Lord." †. Grant
it were fo; to perform, by agreement, a piece of lawful
work for any mafter, whether he be righteous or wicked,
is one thing; and to pray for civil rulers, in the manner
juft mentioned, is another. Upon the fuppofition, that
Cefar was one of the froward princes, or a tyrant and
ufurper; did the precept enjoin the faints in his houfehold, to pray for a blefling, for long life and profperity
to him as fuch, or in his official capacity ? If you can
prove, that it did, it will be fomething to the purpofe;
but any thing elfe is entirely foreign to Mr. Steven's
complaint upon the Loyalift, for comprehending both
the gentle, and the froward prince, within the precept
and example.

Mr. Steven muft be charged with another mifreprefentation; becaufe he confiders the Loyalift as firft fab-
ricating this odd fenfe of Mat. xxii. 21. " That Cefar's
due, by the divine law, was a halter and a gallows,"
and then palming it upon the Reformed Prefbytery. ‡
But whether this be a mifreprefentation, or a well-
grounded complaint, we fhall fee immediately. The
Prefbytery fay, " That by looking into the divine law,
the Jews might fee that Cefar had a juft title to all
that was due to an ufurper, idolater and murderer." ||
Mr. Fletcher fays, " According to them, the fenfe of this
text is, Render therefore unto Cefar a halter and a gallows; which is a forbidding to give tribute to Cefar with
a witnefs." ‡ Says Mr. Steven, " If the fenfe of our
Lord's words, which you mention, is a very odd fenfe,
it is altogether your own; and why fhould you palm
your

---

your own oddities upon the Reformed Prefbytery? It is felf-evident to every judicious mind, that the Prefby: tery, in your quotation, is not fpeaking of our Lord's words concerning tribute at all, but of the divine law as diftinct from them, and given hundreds of years be: fore our Lord's incarnation; by looking into which, and without afking him, they could have known what was Cefar's due." † After giving this fair ftatement of the matter, in the very words of the feveral authors; it would be infulting the underftanding of the judicious reader, to occupy, his time, in proving the juftnefs of Mr. Steven's complaint. But fays Mr. Fletcher, in his own defence, " If Cefar's due was that of a murderer, he certainly deferved a halter, or fome other inftrument of death." ‡ Be it fo: teaching in fo many words, even fuppofing the Prefbytery had done fo, that death was Cefar's due, according to the divine law, is a very different thing from faying, that our Lord, in his reply to the captious queftion, actually fpecified the verdict of the law, and told the Jews, that it was THEIR DUTY, to put Cefar to death, by fome means or other. The Prefbytery, or any other teachers in Ifrael, might fafely fay, that death, according to the law of Mofes, was due to the woman taken in adultery. But it would be fomething very different, and not quite fo confiftent with the truth, to fay, that our Lord, in his reply to thofe who interrogated him on the fubject, actually fpecified this verdict of the Mofaic law, and authorized them to put her to death. The mifreprefentation, there- fore, is evidently on our opponent's fide. But, after all, what can Mr. Fletcher mean, by queftioning this doc- trine of the Reformed Prefbytery, " That Cefar had a juft title unto all that was due to an ufurper, idolater and murderer?" Rather than drop the quarrel, will he rife up in oppofition to the moft ftubborn, and well. authenticated facts? Will he contradict the very Oracles of Heaven? If good hiftory can be fuftained, as the voucher of any fact; unqueftionably Cefar bore the characters, which are here given him. And if the Bible

be

† Let. p. 97. ‡ Def. p. 62.

be true; it is a divine law, no lefs unqueftionable, "Whofo fheddeth man's blood, by man fhall his blood be fhed."† Muft the purple, the crown, and the fceptre be confidered as exempting the criminal, from being obnoxious to the execution of the divine law!

Reprefenting the Loyalift as teaching, "That Chrift finned in paying tribute to the temple," is charged as another of Mr. Steven's mifreprefentations. In oppofition to which Mr. Fletcher replies, "The Loyalift never faid, that Chrift finned, in paying tribute either to Cefar or to the temple; and therefore it is not his, but your own doctrine." ‡ I firmly believe, that it was never the doctrine, neither of Mr. Fletcher nor of Mr. Steven, that ever Chrift, who was holy, harmlefs, undefiled and feparate from finners, could poffibly fin, either in one inftance or another. And it is matter of regret, that ever an idea fo very indelicate and fhocking fhould be fuggefted. Mr. Steven, in the place quoted, confiders it as undeniably evident, that the tribute, paid at Capernaum, was facred and not civil tribute; a pofition which his opponent does not indeed venture to refufe. He views it as no lefs evident, that our Saviour actually paid it to the facred purpofe, for which it was originally intended by the divine law. And therefore Mr. Fletcher's infinuating, "That it was no lefs finful to pay tribute, for fupporting a church, that was wallowing in the mire of error and immorality, than to pay it for fupporting a Pagan civil government," he confiders, if we apply it to the cafe before us, as having a tendency to "Entangle the Lord of Glory in a finful dilemma;" in as much as he muft have paid it for one or other of thefe purpofes. Whether or not the complaint be juft, the impartial reader may judge. But if Mr. Fletcher be truly perfuaded, that there could be no harm in the fimple payment of tribute, for the fupport, either of a Pagan civil government, or of a corrupt church; how is it that he frequently charges Diffenters with contradicting their profeffion by their practice, while

† Gen. ix. 6.   ‡ Def. p. 63.

while they bear, and groan under, the common public
burdens, impofed upon the nation?

The candid reader will certainly be not a little furprifed, to find it alfo, in the fame page, put to the fcore
of mifreprefentation, for Mr. Steven to fay, concerning
the rulers, or rather tyrants of Babylon, " That their
government, inftead of being a bleffing to the captives,
was, from beginning to end, a fcene of violence, tyranny
and oppreffion." A truth which, I apprehend, was
fcarcely ever called in queftion before. The very
names, Perfecutors, Adverfaries, Enemies and Spoilers
of God's people,† with others of the fame kind, whereby
the Spirit of truth characterifes them, plainly fignify fo
much. Thefe, furely, are not empty founds, unmeaning
epithets. Befides, the nature and defign of the captivity
itfelf, proclaim the doctrine. Both fuffering Ifrael, and
the God of Ifrael, viewed it in the light of a grievous
punifhment; inflicted on account of fin, and through
the inftrumentality of the Babylonifh defpots; who
were the tremendous rod of JEHOVAH's anger, and the
terrible ftaff of his indignation, to fcourge and chaftife
a guilty people. In order to accomplifh the awful
defigns of an offended God, it was requifite that the
Babylonians fhould be permitted to exercife their cruelties; till fuch time as he might be pleafed to turn away
his anger and his fury from Jerufalem the holy city;
and make the cup of his wrath to pafs over unto Babylon, in her turn. In exhibiting to our view this fcene
of violence and proud fcorn, the beloved Daniel, nigh
the clofe of the captivity, has this expreffive language,
" The curfe is poured upon us, and the oath that is
written in the law of Mofes. — God hath confirmed his
words which he fpake againft us, by bringing upon us
a great evil.—For our fins, and for the iniquities of
our fathers, Jerufalem and thy people are become a reproach to all that are about us." ‡ By this it appears
to have been the iron rod of oppreffion, under which
they had been groaning, even until the end of the feventy
years.

† Lam. i.   Pfal. cxxxvii. 3.   ‡ Dan. ix. 11,—16.

years. " But there might be, at times, a comparative eafing of their captivity, or fome inftances of mitigation." Be it fo; one or two fmall exceptions were never confidered as deftroying the force of a general rule; otherwife, the Scripture itfelf would oftentimes be exceptionable: . That the Lord, according to the true fcope and fpirit of the paffages cited in the Defence, * made his people to be pitied of all thofe who carried them captive; when, having accomplifhed his holy defigns upon them in Babylon, he gathered them from among the Heathen, and returned their captivity, as ftreams of water in the South, was never denied; nor doth it, in the leaft, militate againft Mr. Steven's affertion. But fays Mr. Fletcher, " The Ifrael of God would have been cut off from being a nation, if the government of the Babylonians had, from beginning to end, been a fcene of violence, tyranny and oppreffion." † An affertion rather too rafh, I apprehend. Concerning the fons of Jacob, in the houfe of bondage, the divine teftimony is, That their cruel lords fhould " afflict them four hundred years." ‡ Or, according to the fpirit of the nervous original, fhould hear and anfwer their complaints, under their grievous oppreffion, by heavy ftrokes, or fevere corrections. If ever a fcene of violence, tyranny and oppreffion was opened in the world, it was certainly in the land of Egypt. But was the Ifrael of God, even under this perfecution, continued for a much longer fpace than feventy years, cut off from being a nation? No; " The more they afflicted them, the more they multiplied and grew." It was the fame church, or people of God, collectively confidered, who were the fufferers in Egypt, and in Babylon. It was the fame God of Jefhurun, who watched over them, in both places, and preferved them from utter deftruction; even in the midft of the furnace. While his hand was not fhortned, that it could not fave, nor his ear heavy, that it could not hear; there was no need to fuppofe, that even violence,

tyranny

* p. 64. † ibid. ‡ Gen. xv. 13.

tyranny and oppreffion, could cut off his people from being a nation. Were it impoffible for a people, collectively confidered, to exift, during the fpace of feventy years, even amidft a fcene of violence and oppreffion; we muft have heard of many more annihilations, under the arbitrary, defpotic, and tyrannical governments, that have been in the world. The fame reafoning will apply to the following paragraph in the Defence, concerning the Roman Emperors. Though there might be a few exceptions; their government, in general, was certainly oppreffive and tyrannical. Others befides Diffenters have thought fo, " The emperors were generally monfters, abandoned to every vice of which human nature is capable. They tyrannized over their fubjects in fuch a manner, that the foldiers, who ought to have been the fervants of the ftate, became its mafters; and inftead of protecting and defending the empire from the barbarous nations around it, fought only to enrich themfelves by its fpoils." † And, by the by, there is no fuch expreffion, neither in the quoted page, nor in any other part of Mr. Steven's Letter as this, that " All the Roman Emperors were a rabble of monfters, without excepting any one of them." The exprefs words are, "—Tiberius, Caligula, Claudius, Nero, and the rabble of the fucceeding monfters." ‡ That is, if we allow the words a fair conftruction, all the reft, of the fame defcription, who came after them. A mode of expreffion, which might fafely be ufed, even fuppofing there had been an equal number of a different character. Whether " Algernon Sidney," from whom the quotation is taken, " was, according to Mr. Steven, a learned gentleman; or, according to others, a learned Deift," doth not at all affect the merits of the caufe. Perhaps it is poffible for the fame perfon to be both thefe. Only one thing is noticeable, that if an author be produced, on the fide of Diffenters; we may always expect him to be ftigmatized with fome mark of reproach or other. I fhall not, at prefent, litigate the matter, with refpect to

† New Edin. Geogr. Vol. I. p. 78.   ‡ Let. p. 37.

to the author in queftion. A few of his own words, however, may be quoted. Speaking of the Ifraelites as not being obliged to have any king; and teaching, that they could not, without a crime, have any but one, who muft not raife his heart above the reft of them; he fays, " This was taught by Mofes: And Samuel, who fpake by the fame Spirit, could not contradict him." † Whether it be the manner of the Deift, to confider holy men of God, living in diftant periods, both fpeaking as they were moved by the Holy Spirit, and having their pens infallibly guided by the wifdom which ᷟcometh from above; the reader may judge. Meanwhile, might we be allowed to afk Mr. Fletcher, what hath become of his charity, which thinketh no evil; efpecially concerning thofe who are no more, to anfwer for themfelves?

Our attention is next turned to " Manifeft contra-dictions." Mr. Fletcher confiders much of his oppo-nent's Letter as confifting of thefe; and is tempted to think that it was written by feveral perfons, not of one mind; and put to the prefs by one as deftitute of ability, as any of them. ‡ Whether he fays fo, on the footing of any furmifes, which he may have heard to that pur-pofe; or if the idea natively rofe in his own mind, on reviewing the contents of the Letter; it is not my pro-vince to fay. But as to the fact; he may be informed, that the Letter is entirely the production of the Author, whofe name it bears. I hope, I may venture to add, that any perfon, deftitute of prejudice, and poffeffing a very moderate fhare of difcernment, with refpect to the peculiarities of ftyle and mode of expreffion, may eafily perceive, even at firft glance, that it is wholly of a piece; and that the Author's manner pervades every fentence of it. Let us attend to the fuppofed contra-dictions.

Concerning the much litigated text, Mat. xxii. 21. Mr. Steven had faid, " Chrift, in general, teaches to give

† Difc. on Gov. Chap. III. Sect. 3. p. 264. Fol. Edit.
‡ Def. p. 65.

give Cefar all things, that by the law of God were due
to him."—And, in the fame page, adds, " The Reformed
Prefbytery juftly deny, that Chrift, in his anfwer to the
fpies, ftated either Cefar's due, or God's due." †—
" You will eafily fee, Sir," fays Mr. Fletcher, " that
thefe fayings, like the legs of the lame, are not equal." ‡
We do very eafily fee, Sir, that they are not equal.
We find it alfo very eafy, and very juft, to obferve,
that he muft fee very ill indeed, who would either mean
or fuppofe them to be equal. The one is a general,
and the other a particular propofition. But there are
many things which are not equal; and, at the fame
time, are not contradictory. A minifter's inftructing
his people, to do juftly, in all things in general, and
give every one his own, is not equal to his particularly
fpecifying, in certain given cafes, what really is every
one's own. Yet the one of thefe he may do; and, for
the time, leave the other undone, without the leaft
fhadow of contradiction. And he who gives a narrative of his procedure, in fuch a cafe, might, with perfect confiftency, fay, He taught in general, that we
fhould give every one his own; but, for reafons which
he could eafily affign, he did not think it neceffary,
at that time, particularly to fpecify, neither what was
his own, nor what was our own; but left us to learn
thefe from other fources of information, to which we
had ready accefs, and with which we profeffed to be
well acquainted. Thus might the narrator of the fact,
in the very fame fentence, or, as Mr. Steven, in the fame
page, pofitively affirm one thing, and deny another,
without the fmalleft contradiction. Were he both to
affirm and deny the fame thing; the matter, indeed,
would be very different. If Mr. Fletcher refufe this
doctrine, in the cafe before us; it muft be at the expence of involving himfelf, inextricably, in the fnare,
with refpect to the other branch of the text. That our
Saviour, in his anfwer, exprefsly taught, in general,
that they were to give God whatever was his due, is

as

† Let. p. 96.　　‡ Def. p. 65.

as plain as words can make it. And that he did not, in his anſwer, at that time, ſpecify what was God's due, is every whit as plain. " Are theſe ſayings, like the legs of the lame, not equal ?" Muſt they alſo rank in the claſs of " manifeſt contradictions?"

It is alſo conſidered as a contradiction, firſt to " aſſert that magiſtracy is an ordinance of God as Creator;" and then to ſay, " There is not the remoteſt hint in Scripture of any other power or dominion exerciſed, in the kingdom either of providence or of grace, but that which is delegated to Chriſt." Here Mr. Fletcher declares, " The laſt of theſe ſayings gives the lie to the firſt." † But it is equally eaſy both to ſay and to prove, that the laſt of theſe is perfectly conſiſtent with the firſt; yea, and conſiſtent too with the rational modes of thinking and ſpeaking amongſt men, not inferior in diſcernment and accuracy, either to Seceders or Diſ- ſenters. The mere delegation of a power, with reſpect to the more immediate exerciſe of it, in order to ac- compliſh ſome important end, whether it be verſant about the appointing of magiſtrates, or any thing elſe, was never, I apprehend, conſidered, by any ſenſible writers on government in general, as the deſtruction or ſwallowing up of that power, in reſpect of the original poſſeſſor. Had this been the caſe; we ſhould not have heard of deputed rulers; or of a viceroy, managing the whole affairs of a kingdom, over which he is ſet by his lord and maſter; who is ſtill, notwithſtanding the delegation of his power, as to the preſent exerciſe of it, to be conſidered and acknowledged as the rightful ſove- reign of that kingdom. Mr. Fletcher, it is hoped, will not refuſe, that God, as Creator and Great Moral Go- vernor, is the Righteous Judge of all the earth; yea, and that this is an eſſential right or power, of which it is abſolutely impoſſible he can ever be diveſted. Neither will he refuſe, that " The Father judgeth no man ; but hath committed all judgment to the Son.—And given him authority to execute judgment alſo, becauſe he is the

† Def. p. 66.

the Son of man." † The extent of the power is abundantly plain. The holy management and righteous
control, given, or delegated, to the Mediator, extend
to heaven, earth, and hell. ‡ " Do you really think,
Sir, that the effential judging-power of the Three-One-
God, is fwallowed up in Chrift's mediatorial power of
judging the quick and the dead ?" One who wifhes to
difmifs the argument, without ever touching it, may
very likely object, "you have compared the King of
kings to earthly rulers, and their deputies." We have
done no fuch thing. But we have fhewn, that the confiftency of delegating power, as to the prefent exercife
of it, without deftroying it in the original poffeffor, may
be argued from cafes amongft men. In other refpects,
there may be fome, or there may be no comparifon ;
notwithftanding any thing we have faid. It may ftill
be objected, " Thofe things are affirmed of Chrift, not
as Mediator, but as God equal with the Father." But
if this be fuppofed to relieve from one abfurdity ; it leads
into another, inconceivably greater. To fpeak of COM-
MITTING or GIVING to Chrift, any power or authority,
fimply confidered as God ; would be very incongruous
indeed ! In that capacity he is abfolutely uncapable of
any fuch gift ; being naturally, eternally and neceffarily
poffeffed of all power, in common with the other adored
perfons of the Trinity. Unwilling to be convinced by
any means, fome may even yet object, and fay, " That
the ruling, controlling, and judging power, afcribed to
Chrift, as Mediator, is confined to the church alone,
and doth not extend to any other part of JEHOVAH's
dominions." The Scriptures cited fully prove the contrary. Befides, even fuppofing it were the cafe ; it
would be no falvo. Hath not the Three-One-God an
effential power of ruling and judging his worfhippers ?
But if the delegation of the power, be equivalent to the
deftruction, or fwallowing of it up, in refpect of the original poffeffor ; the abfurdity will be much the fame,
whe-

† John v. 22. 27.
‡ Mat. xxviii. 18. 1 Cor. xv. 27. 1 Pet. iii. 22. Rev. i. 18.

whether this be the cafe, only in a part, or in the whole
of the dominions. † The doctrine of the quotation from
Mr. Bolton, Diffenters firmly believe, and uniformly
teach; and that in full confiftency with all that either
Mr Steven, or any of his brethren, ever faid.

Mr. Fletcher likewife finds a contradiction between
faying, That magiftracy is not a gofpel ordinance; and
yet teaching, That it is inftituted in the Word. Mr.
Steven had refufed, that either the Reformed Prefbytery,
or any of their followers, ever taught that magiftracy
was a gofpel-ordinance; and fuppofed, that the man
who would make fuch an inference behoved to expofe
either his own ignorance or difhonefty. " The Loyalift,
Sir," fays Mr. Fletcher, " will venture to make the inference, and yourfelf being judge, will neither expofe
his ignorance nor difhonefty. The Reformed Prefbytery have taught, that God Almighty—hath inftituted,
in HIS WORD, the office and ordinance of civil government. Now, Sir, if the ordinance of civil government
be inftituted in the Word, the inference is inevitable,
That Magiftracy is as much a gofpel-ordinance, as
preaching the Word and baptifm, &c. for gofpel-ordinances are to be found, not in the Book of Nature, but
in the Volume of Revelation." ‡ I fhould be very forry,
indeed, to admit the thought, that Mr. Fletcher is
either ignorant, or difhoneft in his intentions. But
there is no faying into what abfurdities the heat of difpute will precipitate fome men. Becaufe gofpel-ordinances are to be found only in the Sacred Volume; how
it will follow, that therefore all other things, which are
found there, muft alfo be gofpel-ordinances, very few,
I prefume, will ever be able to fee. The fallacy of the
reafoning, and its ftriking refemblance to the producti-
ons of ignorance, are fo very evident, that he may run
who reads them. The argument proceeds wholly upon
the very chimerical fuppofition, that there is nothing
other to be found in the Word, befides gofpel ordinances.
Could

† See Henry on Pfal. xcvii. 1. And on Pfal. xcix. 1.
‡ Def. p. 67.

Could this be once eſtabliſhed ; the reſt would, indeed, follow of courſe. The argument would ſtand fair ; and might be thus expreſſed : There is nothing other to be found in the Word, beſides goſpel-ordinances : but magiſtracy is to be found in the Word ; therefore magiſtracy is a goſpel ordinance. Here, however, the firſt propoſition is evidently falſe ; and therefore the laſt, being the concluſion natively drawn from it, muſt be of the ſame deſcription. In the written Word we find the inſtitution of marriage, genealogies, hiſtcries, judicial laws, relative-duties, &c. Are theſe as much goſpel-ordinances as preaching the Word and baptiſm ? We ſhall, likely, be told, Though theſe things be found in the Word ; they are not inſtituted in it. Marriage, however, is certainly inſtituted there, in ſo many words. † But let us not quarrel about found; if the ſubſtance be granted. Neither let us ſhelter ourſelves, as Mr. Fletcher frequently doth, under the covert of doubtful and unexplained terms. When we aſſert, that magiſtracy is inſtituted in the Word ; our meaning is plainly this, That JEHOVAH, the Great Moral Governor of the univerſe, hath, by his Holy Spirit ſpeaking in the Scriptures, made it clearly known, as his will unto his people, that there ſhould be civil government amongſt them; preſcribed the qualifications of the ruler; expreſſly declared, what are the important ends of his office ; and given general rules, for directing his conduct, in his official capacity. ‡ Whoever, then, means to do the argument juſtice ; muſt either ſay ſo too ; or poſitively deny, and aſſign his reaſons.

Adopting the ſentiments of his brother, the author of " The Preſbyterian Covenanter diſplayed," Mr. Fletcher conſiders the doctrine, That magiſtracy is appointed in the written Word, as " pregnant with abſurdities.— Eraſtianiſm in the abſtract.—Groſsly Popiſh.—And neceſſarily leading to this concluſion, That the Heathen world

† Gen. ii. 24. comp. Mat. xix. 5, 6. and Eph. v. 31.

‡ Deut. xvi. 18. with Rom. xiii. 1.—2 Sam. xxiii. 3.— Rom. xiii. 3, 4.—Deut. xvii. 14,—20.

world can have no magiftrates, nor ever could; becaufe they wanted divine revelation : So that this principle at once cuts off the far greater part of the world from a poffibility of having magiftrates." † That the moft precious doctrines in the Bible are capable of being abufed, by wicked and unreafonable men, to favour the abfurdities of Eraftianifm, Popery, and what-not; was never queftioned by us. But this is no proof, that they have any bad tendency, in themfelves. To give the objection all its force, let us fuppofe, though it is no doctrine of ours, that magiftracy flows from Chrift as Mediator, and that he hath appointed the civil magiftrate, as well as the gofpel minifter; ftill it is difficult to fee, how it follows, that the one muft neceffarily ftep into the other's place ; while the offices are perfectly diftinct in themfelves. Upon the fame principle, we behoved to conclude, that becaufe the Deacon and the Paftor are both appointed by the fame Head of the church therefore the duties of their refpective offices muft be blended together. It is true, the blending of two ecclefiaftic offices, is one thing; and the blending of a civil and an ecclefiaftic office, is another. The one, however, is inconfiftent and abfurd, as well as the other. But as the doctrine, That magiftracy flows from Chrift as Mediator, is none of ours ; and as we have ever been ftrenuous oppofers of Eraftianifm, viewing that as one of the principal errors againft which our Teftimony is pointed; we are not accountable for the confequences, neither of the one, nor of the other. To teach, that Chrift, as Mediator, hath a delegated power, to manage, direct and over-rule magiftracy, in fubferviency to the interefts of his church, is a very different thing from teaching, that the ordinance itfelf originally flows from him, in the fame capacity, as the fountain of magiftratical power. The former we hold ; the latter we pofitively refufe.

"If magiftracy is inftituted in the word," fays our opponent, "then the Heathen world can have no magi ftrates."

† Def. p. 68.

ſtrates." But how the one of theſe neceſſarily follows from the other, it is not eaſy to diſcern. Cannot the ſame things, ſometimes, be found, both in the law of nature, and in the written Word? Though the Heathen cannot have any clear, full, or adequate underſtanding of either religious or civil inſtitutions, wanting the light of divine revelation; may they not have ſome obſcure and imperfect knowledge of both? Becauſe we find religious worſhip inſtituted in the Word; muſt we, therefore, conclude, that the Heathen can have no ſort of religious worſhip amongſt them? No, indeed. The inviſible things of God, from the beginning, are ſo made known by the things which are made, that they are ſaid to be without excuſe, for their idolatrous worſhip. We find many volumes written on natural religion. But it will be ſaid, "Their religious worſhip is very imperfect." It is certainly true. And their civil go‑vernment muſt be ſo alſo; while wanting the unerring ſtandard, to direct them. Marriage, as we have juſt ſeen, is inſtituted in the Word; can the Heathen world, therefore, have no marriage amongſt them? Relative duties are very fully, and clearly, preſcribed in the Holy Scriptures; does this ſay, that the Heathen can‑have no underſtanding of the duties, which the parent owes to his child, or the maſter to his ſervant? They who have read the practical works of Cicero, Seneca, and other moral writers among them, will ſoon ſee the contrary. I have often been made to wonder, what our Seceding Brethren could diſcern, ſo remarkably peculiar and odd, about civil government; that they always conſider the light of nature as ſufficient to direct men, with reſpect to the proper requiſites of it; while they never ſpeak of this being the caſe, with reſpect to any thing elſe, which concerns the moral conduct of men. To me it appears, that ſuch a diſtinction is very ill founded. The true ſtate of the matter ſeems rather to be, That although the Heathen, without the aid of the Inſpired Oracles, may have ſome confuſed notions of both civil and religious duties; yet, labouring under this diſadvantage, they cannot have proper, con‑

P   ſiſtent, fiftent, nor adequate ideas of either. Some of the things, which they do, may, materially confidered, be good and commendable ; yet their conduct in general, formally confidered, as clothed with all its circumftances, and viewed in the light of Divine Revelation, muft be exceedingly defective. Mr. Fletcher declares, it is very abfurd to teach, that magiftracy is inftituted in the Scripture. But it is furely much more abfurd, to teach, that it is not inftituted there. If not in the Scripture; where is it inftituted at all ? He will reply, " In the law of nature."—Important difcovery! The law of nature, it feems, is more full and extenfive than the law of the Scripture, comprehending at leaft one inftitution, which is not to be found in all the Bible. And that too, a very precious and interefting inftitution; which, from the very nature and defign of it, neceffarily embraces, in one fhape or other, the whole duties contained in, what is ordinarily called, the fecond table of the moral law.

To prevent miftakes, and throw additional light on this part of the fubject, I beg leave to offer a few remarks, concerning the divine law, by which the faith and practice of men fhould ever be regulated. By a law, in general, we underftand, The righteous will of a lawful fovereign ; made known to his fubjects, by fome means or other, as the regulating ftandard of their conduct. Jehovah, being the Great Sovereign of heaven and earth ; his will, made known to his reafonable creatures, muft be the univerfal law, by which they are all bound. Hence it is plain, that the moral law, fubftantially confidered, being only a tranfcript of his moral image, muft be abfolutely unalterable; though its particular precepts are to be actually applied, agreeably to the diverfified fituations, in which mankind may be placed. Yea, even a pofitive, or ceremonial law, cannot be altered, except by him, who is the Author of it. And therefore, till he fignify his pleafure, concerning its abolition, it muft bind the confcience of the moral agent, as inviolably as the other. Thus it would appear, that the term, Law of Nature, rather

denotes

denotes the particular mode of revelation; than any specific difference in the law itself. Still the will of God, through whatever medium it be made known, muſt be conſidered as the rule of duty. In man's ſtate of primitive integrity, the will of God was written, in very legible characters, on the fleſhly tables of his heart; inaſmuch as he was created after the image of God, in knowledge, righteouſnefs, and true holineſs. This good and acceptable will of God, thus made known, might properly be called the moral law, in reſpect of its perpetual and inviolable obligation. But it might be called the law of nature, in reſpect of the manner, in which it was revealed; man having a clear diſcovery of it, by the unerring dictates of his underſtanding and conſcience; agreeably to the perfect rectitude of his holy nature. Ever ſince the fall, depravity hath pervaded all the faculties of the ſoul; conſequently, the eye, by which the law ſhould be diſcerned and read, hath now become dim. There ſeem, however, ſtill to remain ſome impreſſions of right and wrong; or, in other words, ſome obſcure intimations of Jehovah's will, by the dictates of natural reaſon, and by the conſcience accuſing, or excuſing. But if we call theſe dictates the law of nature; it is evident, that we uſe the term in a looſe and improper ſenſe, for the medium, through which the law is, partly made known. The dictates of any man's judgment or conſcience, even ſuppoſing them to be right, and ſuppoſing you mean them to be only a ſubordinate ſtandard; yet can be a law only to himſelf; but to no other; unleſs you allow one to be the lord of another's conſcience: which would be an encroachment on the divine prerogative. Beſides, theſe dictates are ſo exceedingly diverſified, and contradictory, at different times, and in different men; that they can never poſſibly be any proper and conſiſtent law to the whole ſpecies; neither in one capacity, nor another. The great primary law, therefore, or firſt original ſtandard, by which all human ſocieties, whether civil or religious, ſhould ever be careful to regulate their conduct, muſt ſtill be the will of God; revealed

unto

unto them, in fome form or other. But the Holy
Scriptures are, unqueftionably, the fulleft and faireft
copy of this revelation, that ever was enjoyed, by fallen
man; therefore, the ordinance of magiftracy, if to be
found any-where, muft certainly be found in them. If
any chufe to call the will of God, the law of nature, on
account of its being partly made known by the works
of creation and providence; ftill we are brought to the
fame conclufion. The law is always the fame. The
difference lies only in the medium of difcerning it.
And however full the intimations, through this medium,
may be; they cannot be, fubftantially, different from
thofe contained in the Scriptures; nor is it poffible,
that they can be fo complete. " The heavens," indeed,
" declare the glory of God, and the firmament fheweth
his handy-work. Day unto day uttereth fpeech, and
night unto night fheweth knowledge." But ftill the
Volume of Infpiration, more completely, ferves, " For
doctrine, for reproof, for correction, for inftruction in
righteoufnefs; that the man of God may be perfect,
thoroughly furnifhed unto all good works." Thofe
refpecting his conduct in civil fociety not excepted.

After all, it is truly aftonifhing, that one, who gives
the title of Scripture Loyalist, to his performance;
and complains upon his opponents for " fupporting their
political principles fo much by Acts of Parliament, and
fo little," as he fuppofes, " by the Word of God;" †
fhould be fo exceedingly averfe to this doctrine, That
magiftracy is inftituted in the Word. To confider the
Bible as directing our fubjection to an inftitution, which
is not to be found, from beginning to end of it, muft
certainly appear rather ftrange.

But fays Mr. Fletcher, " If magiftracy is a gofpel-
ordinance, whence is it, that the Reformed Prefbytery,
and their followers, have never obferved it?" ‡ Anfwer,
If once they think it neceffary to teach the doctrine;
they will, probably, attend to its native confequences.
As yet, they have nothing to do, either with the one or
the other.

Addreffing

† Loy. p. 76.   ‡ Def. p. 69.

Addreffing himfelf to his opponent, he fays, "Not
a few pages of your Letter are. tarnifhed with the fin
of flander, by which the empire of Satan was erected,
and is preferved among mankind."* And, for inftances
of this, quotes the 71ft. 124th. and 127th. pages.
The inferences drawn, or things alledged, in thefe pages
of the Letter, are confirmed by fair citations from the
Seceders' Defence of their principles, and from the
Loyalift himfelf; together with other reafons, which
are affigned, and to which Mr. Fletcher hath thought it
proper to make no reply. While, therefore, he, and
his affociates, chufe to call them, "Downright calumnies;" we are at equal liberty, to call them, Downright
truths; until the reafons affigned be difproved.

The Section concludes by afferting, that "This
proverb, *Phyfician, heal thyfelf*, is applicable to many
Mafters, in our degenerate Ifrael." † Of that we en-
tertain no doubt: and, by this time, the judicious
reader will, eafily, fee, that the Loyalift may fairly rank
in the honourable lift.

ANIMADVERSIONS ON SECTION V.

This Section is faid to "Contain a Defence of
the public prayers of Seceders for the King, and for all
that are in authority." ‡

After what hath been already advanced, on this part
of the fubject, § it would be improper, to trefpafs much
farther on the reader's patience. A few additional
remarks, therefore, fhall here fuffice. The prayers
defended by Mr. Fletcher, are thus expreffed, "That
God may blefs our fovereign King George, and the
apparent heir of the crown:—that he may be gracious
to the high courts of parliament, in this and the neigh-
bouring ifland, and lead them to proper meafures for
the

* Def. p. 69. † p. 71. ‡ ibid. § See above, p. 77,—82.

the honour of Chrift." * The queftion, then, at iffue, is precifely this, Whether thefe prayers, as thus ex-preffed, whatever may be the private fentiments of the fupplicant, do not, according to the ufual import of language, neceffarily involve an approbation of the conftitution; by which the throne is fupported, and upon the footing of which alone it is, that the King was ever clothed with any of his royal epithets? There is not, furely, any King of Britain, at prefent, either in civil, or in any other things, either to wear the crown, fway the fceptre, or convene the high courts of parliament, but upon the footing of the complex conftitution. If it fhould be accounted weaknefs; Diffenters are indeed fo weak, as to think, that all fuch general and unquali-fied prayers neceffarily imply an approbation of the conftitution, which provides for the ftability of the throne; and are, fubftantially, the fame with a formal oath of allegiance to the fovereign. Nor are they alone, in this opinion; Mr. Fletcher himfelf grants, that " Praying for magiftrates is an act of fubjection to them." † He certainly means, praying in fuch manner as he and his Brethren do. He intends, like-wife, I fuppofe, fuch fubjection, as recognizes the magi-ftrate's title; otherwife, he rather weakens, than ftrengthens his own caufe. Befides, one of his Brethren, who holds the high rank of Profeffor, and who muft know the conduct of the reft, with refpect to this matter, hath pofitively declared, that " All the minifters in the Seceffion, every Lord's day, give the greateft proof that they can give of their loyalty to the fupreme magi-ftrate. They pray for the ftability of his throne, and the profperity of his government.—Should they fwear allegiance to government every week, in the prefence of many hundred witneffes, could they give a better proof of their loyalty?" ‡ The mode of expreffion neceffarily implies, that they could not. A free con-feffion, with refpect to the import of the general prayer. Perhaps we fhall be told, " That, even fuppofing

Seceders

* Loy. p. 28.　† p. 16.　‡ Confid. on Overt. p. 34.

Seceders were actually to fwear the oath of allegiance; this doth not involve an approbation of the complex conflitution." Seceders fhall be allowed to be their own expofitors. " The queſtion is not," fay they, " whether it be lawful for us to fwear the prefent allegiance to the civil government, which the Prefbytery acknowledge they cannot do; feeing there are no oaths to the government, in being, but what exclude the oath of our Covenants, or homologate the united conflitution." † Thus we find, that the general prayers of Seceders, themfelves being the judges, are equivalent to an oath of allegiance ; and, at the fame time, that the oath of allegiance homologates the united conflitution : whether it be a juſt inference, that thefe prayers muſt, therefore, in like manner, homologate the united conflitution, and are inconfiſtent with the removal of its effential parts, fhall be freely fubmitted, to the judicious reader's determination. Meanwhile, Mr. Fletcher, if he chufe, may certainly fee, that the inconfiſtency, or hypocrify, of which his opponent complains, doth not lye between the thoughts of the heart, and the words of the mouth, for concerning the former Mr. Steven never made the fmalleſt pretention to judge; but it lies between the unqualified and general prayers, as given by themfelves, involving an approbation of the conflitution ; and thofe parts of their Teſtimony, in which they refufe the propriety of taking the oaths, and in which they teſtify againſt many fundamental evils in that conflitution, which, according to themfelves, thefe oaths homologate. There is not, therefore, the leaſt occafion, to think, or fpeak, of occupying the heart-fearching Jehovah's prerogative, in pointing out the inconfiſtency, or hypocrify of thefe things. But Mr. Fletcher finds a very ſtrange evafion. " Seceders," fays he, " are not afhamed to approve of the monarchical form of the Britifh Government, nor do they fcruple to pray for the continuance of it." ‡ I hope he doth not mean, to get into the ſtrong hold of " Monarchical Government

† Declar. of Prin. p. 55.   ‡ Def. p. 72.

vernment in the abſtract," without confidering the complex conſtitution, as it actually exiſts. Diſſenters too can approve of a mixed monarchy, as a very good kind of government, in general. The Martyrs, in the reign of James VII. could very eafily have approved the bare monarchical form of the government; tho' they could not approve the monarchical government; as it was then actually framed, and adminiſtred. All this, is a very different thing from the approving of the conſtitution, at large, as comprehending fo many fundamental laws, and conditions of rule; and different from praying, in loofe terms, for a bleſſing on the high courts of parliament; in one of which Diocefan Biſhops are a conſtituent, an eſſential part, without whom, there is no fuch court exiſting in Britain, neither to be approved, nor condemned.

Mr. Steven had faid, that if Seceders' prayers for government had been heard at all, it feemed to have been in the fenfe of the objectors; for the evils of the conſtitution ſtill continued. Immediately Mr. Fletcher exclaims, " Fine reafoning indeed! An Eraſtian conſtitution continues, therefore Seceders have been praying for the continuance, of it." † No, Sir, that hath not the leaſt fhadow of connection with the reafoning, in the quotation. The thing, inferred by Mr. Steven, is not, that Seceders muſt have been praying for this, or the other thing; but the fenfe or view, in which the prayers, actually prefented in the language fpecified, muſt have been heard; if they were heard at all. While Seceders had prayed, for the continuance, and profperity of the government, in general; the queſtion, between them and us, was, Is that prayer conſiſtent with the removal of the evils, in the conſtitution; or does it neceſſarily imply a continuance of thefe evils, along with the conſtitution, of which they are an eſſential part? Seceders maintain the former; Diſſenters the latter. Now, it is not faid, whether the prayer had been actually heard and anfwered, or not. But if we fuppofe

it

† Def. p. 73.

it to have been heard at all; then, fays Mr. Steven, we muſt furely conclude, that it hath been in the latter fenfe; in as much as the ſtubborn faƈt is, that the evils ſtill continue; along with the conſtitution, for the ſtability of which Seceders pray. This is, evidently, the reaſoning of the quotation, from Mr. Seven's Letter. And it is ſo very plain, that there can be no proper excuſe, for our opponent's unaccountable miſreprefentation of it.

As to the quotation, in the next paragraph of the Defence, concerning feparating between the bad man, and his badnefs; if the reader chufe to look into the 24th and 25th pages of the Letter; he will readily perceive, that what Mr. Steven is properly arguing againſt, is praying, in loofe and general terms, for a bleſſing, long life, and profperity to falfe teachers, or wicked and unlawful rulers, as fuch, in their official capacity; and when you have done fo, pretending, that you only meant to exprefs your concern, for the pardon of their fins, redemption of their fouls, and bodily health, conſidering them fimply as men, and finners of the human race. He alfo objeƈts to the feparating between the ruler, and the conſtitution, on the footing of which he holds and exercifes his power, the principles on which the conſtitution is founded, and the articles of which it is compofed. Separating between thefe, as you pretend to do between the bad man, and his badnefs, he indeed confiders as a whimſical deceit. And many more, I apprehend, will be found to be of the fame opinion. Were Mr. Fletcher to try an experiment on the common fentiments of mankind; I am afraid, that the refult would be rather unfavourable. Should he venture, in fome public company, where the crownlawyers are prefent, openly to exprefs his wifh, for the health, happinefs, long life and profperity of the French Direƈtory; it is highly probable, that difagreeable experience might foon teach him, in what light mankind, ordinarily, underſtand fuch public and folemn wiſhes. Yet the conſtituent members of the Direƈtory, even fuppofing the worſt of it, can only be bad men;

P   unto

unto whom we may certainly pray for grace and repentance.

Mr. Steven is next told, That if he know any fecret plots againſt the Britiſh government; he ſhould diſcover them. † But as he ſpeaks not a word about knowing any, in the place quoted, but only recommends it to thoſe, who profeſs ſuch a zealous attachment to the government, to inquire, if there be any; we have, as yet, no concern with the diſcovery. As to the complaint, about the hypocriſy of the Seceders' prayers, it hath been ſpoken to already.

Strongly reprobating the Reformed Preſbytery's mode of prayer, and giving looſe reins to the moſt bitter invective, Mr. Fletcher ſays, " Your praying for grace to your fellow-men of all ranks, and your praying for the vengeance of the Almighty to be inflicted upon your perſecutors to the uttermoſt, is a very contradictory way of praying." ‡ But Mr. Steven never ſaid, that he prayed for the vengeance of the Almighty, on HIS perſecutors. He told, as warranted by the expreſs words of the Holy Spirit, that the captives in Babylon, in their peculiar circumſtances, having a direct revelation from heaven, concerning thoſe, who were, at once, the avowed and irreconcileable enemies of God, and of his church, were to pray for the vengeance of the Almighty, or the execution of his righteous judgments, upon the BABYLONIANS. Which was, ſubſtantially, the ſame with ſaying, " True and righteous are his judgments." In ſuch prayers, we do not conſider the objects of the vengeance, ſimply as fellow-men, nor even as ordinary ſinners, having ſpace for repentance; but we conſider them, formally, as God's avowed and impenitent enemies, devoted to deſtruction. In this view of them, I ſhould expect, that Mr. Fletcher himſelf would ſometimes pray, for the vengeance of the Almighty to be inflicted on myſtical Babylon, or the New Teſtament Antichriſt. Yet the poor infatuated mortal, who bears the name of Antichriſt, is certainly one of our fellow-men,

a

† Def. p. 74.　　‡ P. 75.

a defcendant of Adam, as well as we. Whatever might become of his perfon, were his kingdom and intereft effectually deftroyed; the church's prayers, for his down-fall, would be fufficiently anfwered. Our opponent goes on; "You pray for grace to all who wear crowns, and, no doubt, for grace to the Pope, who wears a triple crown of blafphemies."—To this I make no reply!—It is fufficient to obferve, that it drops from the pen of a "Seceder, who fears God, and who will not render evil for evil, or railing for railing, but contrariwife bleffing." A very odd way of bleffing, to be fure!

In the following page, it is fuppfed, that the prayers of Seceders, and the prayers of Diffenters are fubftantially the fame; in as much as Mr. Steven had granted, "that he pled for grace to his fellow-men of all ranks and degrees, high or low, prince or peafant." "In this prayer," fays Mr Fletcher, "there are no more exceptions of evils, about the King, and the conftitution, than in the prayers of Seceders." Be it fo: but is there any thing, in the prayer, inconfiftent with the removal of fuch evils; or any thing, which, according to the ufual import of language, neceffarily implies their continuance; as we have already found to be the cafe, in the public prayers of Seceders? I fhould rather fuppofe not.

<hr />

ANIMADVERSIONS ON SECTION VI.

This Section, we are told, "Sheweth, that Mr. Steven's anfwers to the Twelve Queries, are almoft all evafions." It is fuppofed, "that the fafety of his caufe lay in evafive anfwers." † But the caufe, pled by Mr. Steven, needs no fuch apology; neither can a writer, of his fuperior talents, for ftrong and conclufive reafoning, be much hurt, by fuch a mean and ungenteel compliment.

The

† Def. p. 77.

The attentive reader will, at once, fee, that the whole of the Section, before us, is, evidently, a recapitulation, looking back upon the contents of the Letter, in general; and containing fome loofe hints, on the manner of anfwering all the Twelve Queries. The moft of the things, therefore, contained in it, have been difcuffed already. It is hoped, however, that our faying fo, will not be confidered as an evafion: declining to do the fame thing twice, is very different from declining to do it at all.

Concerning the complaint of evafion, which is the great burden of the fong, in this part of the Defence, it is worthy of remark, that thofe very things, of which Mr. Fletcher himfelf is, moft glaringly, guilty, are generally the things, concerning which he takes the very firft opportunity to complain, in the moft loud and clamorous manner. Evafion! Evafion! is the grand complaint. But, after carefully weighing matters, the unbiaffed reader fhall be freely left to judge, if it be not made by one, who, though he hath publifhed a firft edition of his Loyalift, then a fecond, with corrections, and confiderable enlargements; and, after thefe, the Defence; yet, notwithftanding, hath, all this while, never written fo much as one fingle fentence, directly on the fubject in queftion; at leaft, on the fubject, concerning which his opponents hold any fentiments, peculiar to themfelves. We have feen it clear, as noon-day, that the fubjection, for which the Loyalift hath, all along, been ftruggling, fpending his whole ftrength, and exhaufting all his ftores of argumentation, is only a fubjection, which his opponents never denied, in fuch cafes of neceffity; a fubjection, which may, and muft be yielded, under any exifting government, obtaining the afcendency; and a fubjection, which, when yielded, leaves us as much in the dark as ever, with refpect to what properly conftitutes lawful authority, all circumftances being confidered; what are the characteriftics of that power, which we muft confider as ordained of God, and to which we fhould be fubject, for confcience' fake, on pain of condemnation; or what

is

is the defcription of a lawful command, which properly
binds the confcience of a moral agent. On this ground
Mr. Fletcher hath ftudioufly fhunned, to meet his
opponents; though repeatedly called to clofe combat.
With what face, then, can he fpeak of evafion? Let
us fee if he himfelf hath not, evidently, evaded all
Mr. Steven's arguments, in general. That he hath
really done fo, fhall be proved, from his own words.
" I chufe not," fays he, " to bear you company, in
the difagreeable employment of groping in the dark,
and in difputing about a fcheme, which you affect to
wrap in obfcurity." And again, " I will not follow
you through your whirlwind of noify and vain declamation." † Let it be carefully obferved, that though
very different names be impofed; yet the fame things
are, evidently, the objects of attention, with both.
What Mr. Steven reckons plain Scripture-doctrine;
Mr. Fletcher, indeed, confiders as a fcheme wrapt up
in obfcurity: what Mr. Steven accounts fair folid reafoning; Mr. Fletcher calls a whirlwind of noify and
vain declamation: ftill, however, the fame things are
meant; though under very different names. Now
Mr. Fletcher honeftly declares, that he hath no intention of accompanying his opponent, in the confideration
of thefe things. And he hath certainly been as good
as his word. No doubt, it is rather difagreeable, to
be feverely toffed, by a ftrong whirlwind.

Another thing, deferving our notice, is, that
Mr. Fletcher makes no proper allowance, for the
different modes of reply; even fuppofing, ever fo direct
an anfwer, to his query, fhould come out, in end.
Becaufe his opponent doth not, as he would have him,
anfwer immediately, yes, or no, to a queftion propofed,
in the moft loofe, and ambiguous terms; he is highly
offended. If his opponent will not juft fay, in fo many
words, 'Chrift gave the Jews no allowance to kill Cefar;'
all is wrong. If obfervations are made, for the purpofe
of throwing light on the fubject, bringing the queftion

to

† Def. p. 11, 12.

to a proper ftate, and preventing mifunderftandings; anon, we hear the clamour of " Evafion—a bundle of erroneous and extravagant notions—putting one ferpent in the room of another—a 'mafter-piece of evafion— things having no more refpeſt to the query, than to the Popiſh doſtrine of baptizing bells, and conjuring fpirits—profound .filence—a complete pafs-over, as uſual." † Whence it is evident, that Mr. Fletcher himfelf would require very · remarkable indulgence, with refpeſt to his peculiar mode of reply; which, ordinarily, is, juſt to call his opponent's arguments, and illuſtrations, by fome different, and rather more forbidding names; and fo to have done with them. With thefe general remarks, we might fafely difmifs this Seſtion altogether; and be lefs liable to reprehenfi-on, for overlooking it, than Mr. Fletcher is, with re-fpeſt to his opponent's Letter. There are, however, ftill a few things in it, which may be noticed.

" In your anfwer to the firſt Query," fays Mr. Fletcher, " you have not mentioned a fingle Covenanter, who re-fufed to obey the King in things lawful, till he became an abfolute tyrant." ‡ But the proper queftion is not, When our worthy Reformers firſt began, openly to re- · fufe obedience, or to difown the exifting authority; they themfelves, Mr. Fletcher, and we, are all agreed in this, that it was their fin, and puniſhment, to bear the yoke of oppreffion fo long as they did. The queftion is, What were, both fooner and later, the formal reafons of their totally rejeſting the then authority? Their own words, as we have feen, affure us, that ufurping a blaf-phemous fupremacy over the church of Chriſt, and invading the civil liberties of the fubjeſt, were the grand hinges, on which the controverfy always turned. And they had generofity enough, to account the former the more grievous of the two; rightly judging, that open difhonours, done to God, can never be properly puniſhed by thofe, who are themfelves deep in the tref-pafs. I have been often, indeed, furprifed to find, that

our

our Seceding Brethren, when confidering the reafons
for rejecting authority, fhould lay fo much weight upon
acting the tyrant, by invading the civil rights of mankind; and fo little upon the molt glaring ufurpation of
the Redeemer's prerogatives, as fole King in Zion.
That they are fincerely grieved, becaufe of fuch Eraftian
encroachments, I charitably believe; ftill, however,
they do not feem to allow them their due weight, as
preponderating reafons, for difowning thefe earthly
powers, who take too much upon them. Mr. Fletcher
complains upon his opponent, for not mentioning a
fingle Covenanter. Mr. Steven fpeaks of the Martyrs,
in general, and plainly fhews, on what reafons they proceeded. Particular Covenanters have now been mentioned, by name;† who totally rejected the then authority; upon, precifely, the fame grounds, on which Diffenters ftate their Teftimony. Many more could be
mentioned, were it needful. But let our opponent firft
tell us, when Charles II. became an abfolute tyrant.
And then we fhall be in readinefs to anfwer, whether it
was before, or after his becoming fuch, that the Martyrs rejected him. Let him favour us with the proper
defcription of fuch a tyrant, as ought, indeed, to be
refifted and rejected by men; and we fhall take it
very kind. For my own part, after ftriking from the
bloody lift, the monftrous, the murdering, and, to ufe
Mr. Fletcher's dialect, " the infernal" Nero; I fhould
be abfolutely at a lofs to find the tyrant, in Charles II.
in James VII. or indeed in any ruler, that ever exifted,
under the fun; either in one period of their reign, or
in another. Yet, according to our author's doctrine,
Nero was not to be refifted, but on pain of condemnation. How comes it, then, that other tyrants, who are
but as the dwarf before the giant, fhould, at any period
of their reign, be refifted, rejected, or depofed? As to
" obeying in lawful commands," the very ambiguous
and evafive mode of expreffion, ordinarily ufed by
Mr. Fletcher, and which properly afcertains nothing,
with

† See above p. 69,—73.

with refpect to the fubject before us, neither *pro* nor *con*;
I fhould reckon it a matter of very little importance,
whether it be done before, or after, the ruler becomes
abfolute tyrant: for, if the queftion be fairly ftated,
I do not fee, how there can be much harm in it,
at any time.

Suppofing it impoffible for Mr. Steven, in anfwering
the fecond Query, to exculpate Diffenters from the
charge, of contradicting their principles, by their practice, Mr. Fletcher inftructs his intelligent reader to afk,
" Why do the Reformed Prefbytery, and their followers,
difown the Britifh Government, and yet fupport it as
much as any of their neighbours, by going to law, by
paying land-taxes, toll, tribute, cuftom?" * Were I to
retaliate, I might afk, Why do Seceders difown Prelacy
and the Bifhops' Courts, in England and Ireland, and
yet fupport them, as much as any of their neighbours, by the Church-payments there? And why does
Mr. Fletcher maintain, that the pofitive command,
as he underftands the text, to pay the tribute unto
Cefar, fays nothing, either directly or indirectly, concerning the recognizing of his authority ; † and yet
fuppofe, that paying toll and tribute, in our times,
neceffarily implies a recognizing of authority?—But
I find this part of the difpute difcuffed, at great length,
by our worthy deceafed friend, Mr. Steven, in his
Second Letter, ‡ publifhed fince his death; to which
I refer Mr. Fletcher, and the reader.—As to the charge,
of borrowing hands from our good neighbours, to do
what we will not do ourfelves, ‖ it hath long fince been
refuted, as a malicious calumny; and therefore merits
no further attention. §

In the 80th page of the Defence there are two affertions, rather difficult to reconcile. " The queftion is
not about the characters, but about the precepts in this
paffage." And in the very next fentence but one,
" The precepts in the firft part of this paffage, muft not
be

* Def. p. 78. † p. 82,--83. ‡ See particularly p. 7,—17.
‖ Def. p. 79. § See Mr. M'Milian's Let. p. 70.

be feparated from the characters in the laft part of it."
If the precepts and characters be infparable; I fhould
apprehend, that difputing about the one, would oblige us
to difpute about the other, at the fame time, and to
take them in connection : as Mr. Fletcher himfelf, indeed, at the end of the paragraph, pofitively declares
we fhould do. That great burden of the fong, " Magiftracy in the abftract," and the doctrine of our Teftimony, concerning Cefar, which are again introduced,
in the two following pages, have been animadverted on
already.

Our grateful acknowledgments are due to Mr. Fletcher,
for his conceffion, That the paffage, *Render to Cafar the
things that are Cefar's*, fays nothing, either directly or
indirectly, about the lawfulnefs of his authority ; and
that it would be fool-hardinefs to attempt a proof of it,
from that part of Scripture. † This text hath all along
been confidered, by Seceders, as the great and impreg-
nable bulwark, for the fecurity of their principles, concerning owning lawful authority, and obeying lawful
commands ; but, according to the conceffion before us,
it would be fool-hardinefs to attempt a proof of the
lawfulnefs of Cefar's authority, from that paffage ; confequently, the obedience, which it enjoins, even fuppof-
fing that the words contain a direct command to pay
the tribute-money, may ftill, for ought at leaft we can
gather from the paffage itfelf, be nothing more than that
paffive fubjection to fuperior force, which neceffity dictates, under any governmet, whether lawful, or unlawful. And indeed the Jews could never poffibly owe any
other fort of fubjection unto Cefar. Hence it is evident, that our opponent's conceffion implies more,
in favours of our caufe, than both the editions of
the Loyalift, and the Defence, put together, can ever
make againft it ; in as much as it, evidently, faps the
very ftrongeft foundations of all the arguments, contained in thefe books.

Mr.

† Def. p. 82, 83.

R

Mr. Fletcher next fpeaks of " An article in the creed of the Reformed Prefbytery, which," fays he, " is exceedingly erroneous, or rather blafphemous. The diabolical article is this, That the accufers of Chrift fpake the truth, when they faid, We found this fellow perverting the nation, and forbidding to give tribute to Cefar." ‡ I am very forry, indeed, that our opponent fhould thus confidently affert, at the expence of truth. But the honour of religion, and the defence of the caufe, which I fincerely profefs, oblige me, pofitively to aver, that there is no fuch article, as that mentioned, neither in the Teftimony, nor in any other writings of the Reformed Prefbytery, from beginning to end; nor any thing which bears the moft diftant fhadow of refemblance unto it. I hope, " our witnefs is in heaven, and our record is on high," that we abhor even the moft diftant thought of admitting, that the accufers of the meek and lowly Jefus fpake the truth, when they faid, " We found this fellow perverting the nation." Yet this makes a part of the propofition. As to the following words, " and forbidding to give tribute to Cefar," Mr. Fletcher knows perfectly well, that the interpretation, given in our Teftimony, refufes, that Chrift either commanded, or forbade to give tribute to Cefar; but teaches, that he left the matter undetermined altogether, as he did in many other cafes, of ftill higher importance; when he found the queftion put, not for the fake of receiving information, but for the purpofe of enfnaring him. Declining to anfwer the captious queftion, agreeably to this interpretation, whether it be reckoned right or wrong, is very different from clearly deciding it, and pofitively forbidding to give tribute to Cefar, as the falfe accufers maintained he did. The text, Luke xxiii. 2. is cited in the Teftimony, folely for the purpofe of proving, that the Jews themfelves did not underftand the words of Chrift as a command to pay tribute; though this would certainly have fuited the prejudices of fome of them, and been fubfervient to

their

‡ Def. p. 83.

their wicked defign. A fingle word, however, there
is not in all the Teftimony, on the queftion, Whether
thefe accufers, in their charge againft Chrift, fpake
the truth, or fpake falfehood; though the latter was
certainly the cafe: and it can be faid in full confiftency
with every iota of our principles. With regard to
that rather fingular mode of expreffion, " diabolical
article," Mr. Fletcher, had he thought it proper, might,
for the fake of the Englifh reader, have given us the
tranflation, and told, that the Teftimony of the Reformed
Prefbytery contained " a blafphemous and devilifh article." If the candid reader fhould have been ftruck
with furprife, at the harfhnefs of the expreffion; he
might have affured him, that it is ufed by " a Seceder,
who fears God, and who will not render evil for evil,
or railing for railing, but contrariwife bleffing; and
who will not offer ftrange fire on God's altar, left he
be confumed." !

On what follows, concerning the approved examples
of the faints, * it would be altogether fuperfluous to
detain the reader, after what hath been faid already. †
Only, I cannot help remarking, on Mr. Fletcher's
very uncandid and abufive manner of quoting from his
opponent. He introduces Mr. Steven faying, " Neither
Mr. Thorburn, nor the Reformed Prefbytery, reject
the approven example of the faints in Scripture; but
they prefer Scripture-precept to the approven example
of the faints." ‡. As thefe words are diftinguifhed by
the ordinary quotation-marks, the reader would certainly expect to find them in Mr. Steven's Letter.
The firft part of the fentence, it is true, we have,
p. 109, 110. But the laft part of it, " They prefer
Scripture-precept to the APPROVEN example of the
faints," is no-where, in all the Letter, to be found;
nor indeed any thing like it. Mr. Steven's words,
and they are the only words, in his reply to the
8th. Query, which Mr. Fletcher can poffibly have
in view, ftand exactly thus: " Mr. Thorburn, in your
quo-

---

* Def. to p. 87.　　† See above p. 66,—68.　　‡ Def. p. 86.

quotation means no more, than a preference of Scripture-precept to the example of the faints, as the divine
standard of all practice, contrary unto, or inconfiftent
with which no example of the beft faint is of any confequence." * So foon as Mr. Fletcher fhall fhew us
the error which this doctrine involves, he may expect
to be attended unto; till then, we muft be allowed
to confider it as perfectly orthodox. The attentive
reader will difcern at once, that, in order to blind him,
and give an entirely different turn to the ftate of the
queftion, the word APPROVEN is artfully foifted into
this part of the fentence, by our opponent.

Speaking of Mr. Steven's anfwer to the ninth Query,
Mr. Fletcher proceeds, " Inftead of faying a fingle word
to this Query, you infult your own, and the underftanding of every fenfible reader, by a railing accufation
againft the Loyalift, as a teacher of the doctrine of
paffive obedience, and as adducing the paffive obedience
of Chrift, as an example having the force of a precept,
and binding the confciences of Chriftians to the defpotic
authority of cruel tyrants. Enough," continues he,
" has been faid in the preceding pages to refute this
calumny." † As we have only bare affertion here;
it is equally eafy for me to reply, while the impartial
reader fhall be left to fay, if it be not juft, That enough
has been faid, in Mr. Steven's Letter, and in the preceding pages ‡ of thefe Animadverfions, to fix, not
indeed the calumny, but the juft charge, upon the
Loyalift; beyond the poffibility of exculpation. That
the Redeemer's meeknefs, under fuffering, exhibited
a noble pattern of patience, and humble fubmiffion, unto
all his people, when they are perfecuted, afflicted, tor-
mented, and find no way of efcape, is readily granted,
on all hands. But that his holy fubmiffion, in that
awful fituation, was ever intended as a determining
ftandard, whereby we are to afcertain that obedience,
which is due, for confcience' fake, to lawful civil authority, is what can never be proved." Mr. Fletcher,

in-

* Let. p. 109. † Def. p. 87, 88. ‡ See from p. 40,—48.

indeed, hath been wife enough not to attempt it. Only, to keep himfelf in countenance, he raifes a mighty out-cry about the fin of reviling the pious Mr. Henry: * a matter, concerning which, he had not the leaft occafion to fpeak a fingle word; in as much as his opponent never dropt the moft diftant hint, injurious either to the memory, or the doctrine of that great man. Mr. Steven, fo far as ever I could learn, put as high a value upon Mr. Henry, as ever Mr. Fletcher needed to do; while, in full confiftency with his own doctrine, he could, chearfully fubfcribe every word of the quotation, alluded to. " The dead," fays our opponent, " are very harmlefs antagonifts, they cannot take unto them the buckler and the fhield." It is very true: and, agreeably to his own doctrine, we fhould have expected, that Mr. Fletcher might fpare the duft of Mr. Thorburn, many years ago, laid in the grave. But perhaps he " only intended to fmite furviving brethren through the loins of a dead man, who could not arife and wipe off the reproach." † In the two following pages, there is nothing, which we have not already confidered, except the remarks, about fupporting our political principles, fo much by Acts of Parliament, and fo little by the Word of God.

Mr. Steven had faid, " The Reformed Prefbytery believe, that they fupport their political principles wholly by the Word of God, even when they call in the aid and authority of Acts of Parliament." ‡ And had affigned his reafons. Mr. Fletcher reckons this inconfiftent, and afks, " If your political principles are wholly fupported by the Word of God, pray Sir, what need is there to call in the aid of Acts of Parliament to fupport them ?" ⸸ The one, however, is no contradiction to the other. Mr. Fletcher and his brethren, it is hoped, fupport the evangelical doctrines, which they believe, profefs and maintain, wholly by the Word of God, as the alone infallible judge, by which all controverfies in religion are to be ultimately, determined; is it, therefore,

* Def. p. 89.   † ibid.   ‡ Let. p. 124.   ⸸ Def. p. 91.

fore, contradictory and abfurd, to call in the aid of Con-
feffions and Catechifms; in order to exprefs, by thefe
mediums, their adoption of the precious doctrines contained in the Word, and their feafonable application of
thefe doctrines, to their own cafe, in their church-capa-
city? I fhould fuppofe not. No more inconfiftent is it
for us, to confider the Holy Scriptures as the alone infallible ftandard, by which our political principles are
to be, ultimately, afcertained, judged, and fupported;
and, at the fame time, to teftify our approbation of the
Reformation-Acts of Parliament, and our ftrict adherence unto them; as agreeable unto the Word of God,
and as the great human bulwark, or outward defence,
of our civil and religious liberties. Taking the revealed
will of God, as the only fure foundation, or warrant,
for all our principles, whether in our civil, or religious
capacity; and yet calling in the fubfidiary aid of human deeds, for protecting, and fecuring unto us the poffeffion of thefe principles, doth not appear to involve
any contradiction.

If we are not to call in the aid of human decrees,
and Acts of Parliament; I fhould like to be informed,
how Mr. Fletcher himfelf came by that civil part of the
Britifh Conflitution, which he highly approves, and
how he afcertained the will of his favourite PRIMORES
REGNI, in excluding a Popifh Pretender; and fecuring
the crown to the Houfe of Hanover, on certain fpecified
conditions. In regulating his views of thefe matters,
he will find himfelf obliged to act, upon the very fame
general principle, with Diffenters, in calling in the aid
of human laws. He muft, no doubt, apply the principle,
to a different object. The Reformation—Acts are our
auxiliaries; while the Revolution-Acts are his. But
we both agree, in the general principle, of feeking
aid from human authority, or public national deeds.
Let our opponent, therefore, give the fame liberty to
others, which he takes to himfelf; and this part of the
difpute is over.

The

The Loyalift goes on, to inform us, "That his political principles are built upon the foundation of the
Apoftles' and Prophets, Jefus Chrift himfelf being the
chief corner-ftone." † Had Mr. Steven, or any of the
Reformed Prefbytery, faid fo; I am afraid, he would
very foon have been told, that he was making magiftracy, or politics, "as much a gofpel-ordinance as
preaching the Word and baptifm." Certain it is, that
in all the writings of Diffenters, there cannot be found
a fingle fentence, which favours fo much of doing fo.
Is the Loyalift alfo among thefe, who find magiftracy
in the Word; who view the neceffary qualifications
of the civil ruler, and the indifpenfible duties of his
ftation, clearly prefcribed, and particularly fpecified
there? No, furely; but, rather than drop the employment of contradiction, he muft, it feems, do and undo,
fay and gain-fay, juft- as occafion requires. If Diffenters maintain, that magiftracy is inftituted in the Word;
then he muft tell them, that fuch doctrine " is pregnant
with abfurdities." If they refer to Acts of Parliament,
in paffing which men may be confidered as acting,
according to the dictates of right reafon, though in
confiftency with the Word; then the Loyalift, who
calls thefe dictates the law of nature, in which magiftracy is founded, is, forthwith, ready to aver, "that he
will not pay fuch a poor compliment to the Holy Scriptures, as to call in the affiftance and authority of human
decrees, for the fupport of his political principles." †
Yea, in fome unguarded hour, when he is not perhaps,
remembering what he hath faid againft D'ffenters, he
will teach nearly, if not exactly their doctrine, com-
plaining upon the " modern advocates for toleration of
grofs herefy, blafphemy, &c." becaufe they " teach,
that Chriftian magiftrates fhould govern their fubjects,
not by the Word of God, but by the law of nature.
It is true," fays he, " that the ordinance of magiftracy,
and that the relation between magiftrates and fubjects,
are founded in the law of nature; but it is impious to
con-

† Def. p. 92.   ‡ ibid.

conclude from this, that the Chriſtian magiſtrate ſhould prefer the ſmoking flax of the light of nature to the burning and ſhining lamp of the revealed will of God ; that he ſhould not have a copy of the written law of God, and read therein all the days of his life, left he ſhould be a Judaizer. This doctrine leads to Deiſm, to a rejection of our Bible." † Very good Diſſenting doctrine ; and expreſſed almoſt in the ſame words, which they have often uſed. They can readily allow, with Mr. Fletcher, that magiſtracy is founded in the law of nature ; while they alſo teach, that it is founded in the law of Scripture ; becauſe they conſider theſe as ſubſtantially the ſame. But the light of nature, by which we have ſome faint diſcernment of the law, is, indeed, a very weak taper, unaſſiſted by Revelation.

In the ſame page, Mr. Fletcher tells his opponent, " you have not, becauſe you could not, mentioned a ſingle text in the Sacred Volume, to prove that it is your duty to diſown the authority of Chriſtian Magiſtrates, who are a terror to evil doers, and a praiſe to them that do well. You durſt not attempt to prove your political principles from the Word of God, becauſe it would have been an attempt to prove, that rebellion, which is as the ſin of witchcraft, is authorized in the Holy Oracles." The reader will, no doubt, be rather ſurprized, to hear Diſſenters blamed, by the ſame author, and at the ſame time, both for finding " magiſtracy inſtituted in the Word ;" and for " not attempting to prove their political principles from the Word." Such ſtrange things, however, are common, in the Defence. The Loyaliſt may thus go on, ſo long as he pleaſeth, to inſult Diſſenters, by impoſing upon them his own abſurd, and ſelf-contradictory ſtates of the queſtion ; but ſo ſoon as he can ſhew, when or where, they ever taught any ſuch doctrine, as that which he here complains they have not attempted to prove ; I hope, they ſhall be in readineſs to adduce the Scripture-proofs. Till then, they will reckon themſelves excuſed, from

ſay-

† Pref. to his Compend of Brown's Letters on Toleration, p. 4.

faying any thing farther, than what hath been faid already, on that part of the fubject. As to the beloved theme, " that rebellion is as the fin of witchcraft," it is vaft pity, that neither Mr. Fletcher, nor any of thofe who have dwelt moft upon it, feem properly to advert to the fcope of the paffage, from which the affertion is taken. It is not the fuppofed rebellion of a people, contending for the purity of God's ordinance of magiftracy; and, even when they cannot obtain it, in fuch ftate as they would wifh, refolving, through grace, to live peaceably with all men, as is the cafe with Diffenters : no; it is the rebellion of a king, againft the exprefsly revealed will of God; the ftubbornnefs of a prince, in rejecting the word of the Lord, acting contrary to the Scriptural and fundamental laws of the kingdom, on the footing of which he, and every king in Ifrael, was to receive and hold his crown, and making forbidden encroachments, on the fpiritual liberties of the church, by prefuming himfelf to offer a burnt-offering; though that work belonged not at all to him, but to ecclefiaftical perfons, called, and appointed of God, for that purpofe. This is the rebellion, evidently, intended; and declared, by the Spirit of God, to be as the fin of witchcraft. * So that this text, in place of making againft Diffenters, is directly for them; and, taken in its true fpirit and fcope, will bear them out; in the fupport and defence of all their political principles.

Concerning Mr. Steven's complaint upon the Loyalift, " for relinquifhing the whole of the civil part of our Reformation;" † it is obfervable, that, as ufual, the Loyalift never fo much as touches one of the reafons, or illuftrations, which his opponent had offered, in fupport of the allegation; but, inftead thereof, raifes a very loud out-cry againft him, for " throwing the dirt of calumny, and murdering his neighbour's character." ‡ A very fhort, and ready way, of difpatching an argument. Had not Mr. Fletcher himfelf affured us, " that he will not offer ftrange fire on God's altar, nor render

rail-

* 1 Sam. xii. 9,—14. & xv. 23. † Def. p. 92. ‡ p. 93.

railing for railing, but contrariwife bleffing;" there are
fome things, in the part of the Defence before us, which
would almoft tempt his reader, to form a different opinion. Mr. Steven is here reprefented, " as murdering
his neighbour's character, under pretence of defending
the truth, which is faid to be no lefs criminal, perhaps,
than the offering of human facrifices to God." The
neceffary inference, with refpect to Mr. Steven, is
abundantly obvious.—But I fhudder at the thought!
and refile from the painful tafk of mentioning it.

Expreffive of his humility, and the fenfe which he
had of his own weaknefs, Mr. Steven had granted,
" that he was not bleffed with a happy capacity of
expreffing his thoughts in a narrow bounds." † " It is
a truth," fays Mr. Fletcher, at the top of this page.
The confeffion, from Mr. Steven, was, evidently, an
indication of great modefty, and diffidence; fomewhat
refembling the Apoftle's acknowledgment, that he was
rude in fpeech; and lefs than the leaft of all faints.
For Mr. Fletcher to take the advantage of it, and add
his amen, is fuch a glaring inftance of ungenteel, and
ill-bred treatment, as is feldom to be met with, amongft
Chriftian writers; and, indeed, is rather below notice.

The mighty triumph over Mr. Steven, in this and
the following pages of the Section, as though he had,
" in one fentence, demolifhed the ftudy and labour of
ten years, and given up the caufe to his antagonift,"
happens to be rather primature; being, evidently,
founded, before the victory be obtained, or indeed the
moft diftant appearance of its ever being fo. The conceffion is, " The Scripture-examples prove, that the
faints, in cafe of neceffity, may be fubject to tyrants
and ufurpers in all things lawful, and yet be blamelefs."
If fo, fays Mr. Fletcher, " Is it not a fair and unavoid-
able conclufion, That faints may be fubject, in all things
lawful, to Chriftian magiftrates, who are neither tyrants
nor ufurpers, and yet be blamelefs?" Moft certainly:
and what Diffenters ever either faid, or thought, otherwife?

† Let. p. 127.

wife? But when all this is granted, they have not renounced fo much as a fingle iota of their avowed principles. The fubjeƈtion, conceded, is only fuch as " neceffity" diƈtates, and as may be yielded to tyrants and ufurpers, who, on account of a people's fins, may be permitted to have dominion over their goods, and their cattle; and to bring them into great diltrefs: but it has no conneƈtion with the recognizing of the ruler's title, nor with afcertaining the lawfulnefs of the conditions, on which he receives, and holds his crown. While thefe are out of the queftion; the doƈtrine, taught by Mr. Steven and his brethren, ftands untouched.

Our opponent alfo exhibits here, another fpecimen of the blefling, which he renders for railing. " The intelligent reader," fays he, " will eafily fee, from the preceding pages, that the leading features of your Anfwers to the Twelve Queries, are mere evafions, mifreprefentations, calumnies, contradiƈtions, vain and naufeous repetitions, raifing the ghoft of paffive obedience and non-refiftance almoft in every page." Beginning to read his opponent's Letter, he finds himfelf " prefently falling in among inveƈtives, calumnies, and filly evafions." † As the bare rehearfal, it is prefumed, may be fufficient, to give the reader an idea of Mr. Fletcher's peculiar way of bleffing; I fhall not, after what hath been faid above, trouble him with any farther remarks.

At the end of the Seƈtion, Mr. Steven is told, " Sir, your paffionate outcries againft the Loyalift, fignify that he hath touched you to the quick." ‡ With refpeƈt to this, it fhall be freely, and without the fmalleft apprehenfion for the confequence, fubmitted to the unbiaffed and judicious reader, on what fide the paffionate outcries are loudeft; and, confequently, where we have the ftrongeft evidence, of being touched to the quick.

† Def. p. 96.   ‡ p. 97.

A N I-

Tнis Section, it is faid, " Sheweth, that Mr. Steven's arguments are altogether infufficient to fupport his caufe." The Loyalift means now " to act offenfively, and to combat the Reformed brethren, with weapons of their own framing." Certain premifes are mentioned, and confidered as exhibiting Mr. Steven's doctrines, and arguments; then we are told, that even fuppofing thefe to be true, this, and the other thing, cannot be inferred from them. †

That not one, in ten, of Mr. Steven's arguments, is ever fo much as mentioned, in this fhort Section, the attentive reader will fee at once; but how they can be fhewn to be inconclufive, without fpeaking a fingle word about them, either good, or bad, will probably remain a myftery to every man, except. the Loyalift himfelf. It is obfervable, that even fome of the pre-mifes, here mentioned, are not to be found at all, neither in the Teftimony, nor in Mr. Steven's pamphlet. As to the things, which, it is faid, will not follow; it is a matter of no importance, in this controverfy, whether they follow, or not. They are, generally, at leaft, fuch things as we never either thought, or faid; yea, fome of them are things, which we very much abhor. But let us meet the fatal weapons of this offenfive war.

" If it were true, as your Teftimony plainly teaches, that Chrift forbade the Jews to give tribute to Cefar, you cannot conclude, from this, that tribute is not due to the Britifh Government." Anf. We have proved before, that the Teftimony teaches no fuch thing. And whether we give, or do not give tribute to the Britifh Government, it fays nothing about recognizing the ruler's authority; Mr. Fletcher himfelf being judge; for if a pofitive command, to give tribute to Cefar fay nothing even indirectly, concerning recognizing his au-thority;

† Def. p. 97, 98, 99.

thority ; obedience to fuch a command, muft neceffarily fay as little. † " Suppofing it to be true," proceeds our Author, " that Cefar had a juft title to all that was due to an ufurper, idolater, and murderer ; you cannot infer from this, that the Britifh Magiftrates are ufurpers, idolators, and murderers, and therefore that—a halter, or a gallows is their due." We never entertained the moft diftant thought of either faying, or inferring any thing of the kind ; nor has this any more connection with our doctrine, than inferring from it, that the fun rifes in the Weft. If Cefar was, indeed, a tyrant and a murderer, as hiftory fully vouches ; what we natively, infer is, that Cefar could have no juft title to the confcientious obedience of the Jews, as their lawful fovereign : the oppofite of which Mr. Fletcher maintains ; elfe, his reafoning is nothing to the purpofe. But he goes on, " If it were true, as you fay, That Chrift did not recognize the power of Cefar as lawful ; it cannot follow, that the authority of the Britifh Magiftrates is unlawful." Be it fo : yet it both can, and muft follow, that the text makes nothing for Mr. Fletcher's purpofe ; for if it prove nothing concerning the lawfulnefs of Cefar's authority ; why does he continually produce it, as a proof, that the prefent Britifh Rulers are lawful Scriptural magiftrates, and ought to be acknowedged as fuch ? That this text afcertains nothing, in fupport of Mr. Fletcher's caufe, is the juft, and the only inference, which, in this difpute at leaft, we need, or mean to draw from our view of it. As to the next inference, " That the Britifh Magiftrates are as bad as the Roman Cefars," it alfo is a doctrine, with which we have no concern, having never taught any thing like it ; and therefore we return it to the inventor, to be difpofed of, as he may find occafion. Mr. Fletcher's opponent muft ftill be told, " If it were lawful, as you very unwarrantably have affirmed, That we fhould pray for violence and the vengeance of the Almighty, to be inflicted upon our perfecutors to the uttermoft ; you cannot reafonably con-

† Sec above p. 118, 119.

conclude from this, that our civil rulers are perfecutors, and that it is lawful to pray for damnation to them." On reading this I can fcarcely refrain from the Pfalmiſt's exclamation, "Wo is me, that I fojourn in Mefech, that I dwell in the tents of Kedar. My foul hath long dwelt with him that hateth peace!" How our friend, Mr. Fletcher, can fatisfy his own confcience, when he thus, knowingly and deliberately, perverts the words of his opponent ; and, under the fanction of quotation-marks, fathers upon him doctrines, which never once entered his mind, nor dropt from his pen, it is hard to fay. " That we ſhould pray for violence, and the vengeance of the Almighty, to be inflicted on our enemies to the uttermoſt," is a doctrine, to which Mr. Steven ever was, and to which all his furviving Brethren ſtill are abfolute ſtrangers."† Nor can they, without juſt abhorrence, admit even the moſt diſtant thought of the unchriſtian, and abominable inference, concerning praying for damnation to the prefent civil rulers. I hope they can, through grace, pray, that the Lord may, in mercy, forgive Mr. Fletcher, and every other man, who fuppofes them capable of any fuch thing. In full confiſtency with all their principles, and with the fafety of their own confcience, they can pray for bodily health, faving grace, and everlaſting happinefs, unto thofe who ' are advanced to be rulers in the nation, as well as unto all others ; though they have no clearnefs to fubfcribe to the footing, on which they hold, and exercife, their regal power. Our opponent proceeds : "If it were a fact, as you fay, without the ſhadow of proof, That our noble army of Covénanters and Martyrs, rejected the authority of the tyrannical royal Brothers ; you cannot, with any ſhadow of reafon, infer from this, that the Britiſh King is a tyrant, and that his authority ſhould be difowned." To this I reply : We have now given, not the ſhadow, but the fubſtance, of inconteſtible proof, that many in the noble army of Covenanters and Martyrs, totally rejected the authority of the tyrannical

royal

† See above p. 84,—88.

royal Brothers, both in civil, and ecclefiaſtic matters. †
It is only of late, indeed, that Seceders themſelves have
begun to deny it. But they are now convinced, it would
feem, that the acknowledgment of it muſt ruin their
caufe ; as certainly it would : for the martyrs were always but a very ſmall minority. As to the inference,
"That the Britiſh King is a tyrant," it is no-where,
fo far as I remember, to be found, in all the writings of
Diſſenters. Mr. Fletcher himſelf being the contriver ;
he alone is accountable, for the propriety, or impropriety, of drawing it from the premiſes. If Diſſenters
ſpeak of difowning authority ; they tell, both in what
fenfe, and for what reaſons. ‡ With regard to Mr.
Fletcher's peculiar manner, of giving other names to
ſtrong arguments, and clofe reaſoning, which he either
doth not chufe to combit, or perhaps cannot very eafily
overturn, calling them, as here, "calumnies, contradictions, falfeoods, and mifreprefentations," and fo difpatching them at once, or telling us what cannot follow
from them ; it hath been animadverted on already, and
deferves no further reply. To give the finiſhing ſtroke;
Mr. Steven is told, "You yourſelf, Sir, muſt fee, if
you are not voluntarily blind, That your caufe is built
on the fand." If it be, indeed, fo ; there could be no
proper occaſion for Mr. Fletcher to fpend fo much time,
and make fo many furious aſſaults, in order to batter it
down. He might have left it to fall, under its own
weight. It is rather furprifing, indeed, that a fabric
built on the fand, ſhould have ſtood fo long. It hath
not, certainly, been for want of tempeſtuous ſtorms,
beating againſt it.

That we may know how Mr. Fletcher means to act,
for the future, he tells his opponent, "If you ſhould
write five hundred volumes on ridiculous and extrane-
ous fubjects, a filent contempt will be the reply of the
Loyaliſt. But if you begin, for you have not yet begun, the matter in debate, which is precifely this, Whe-
obedience is due to the prefent civil Britiſh Government,

† See above p. 70,—75.   ‡ p. 53.

ment, in its lawful commands or not; the Loyalist hath
no objections to fee it out with you, if the Lord give
time, ability, and opportunity." † The much refpected
Author, to whom this language is addreffed, is no more,
to anfwer for himfelf: he hath already both begun, and
finifhed, all that ever he had to do, in this world. But
furviving Brethren may reply for him. If once Mr.
Fletcher begin, for neither he, nor any on his fide of the
difpute, have ever yet begun, to define the terms, and
explain the ftate of the queftion; fome Diffenter or
other may, likely, undertake to meet him, on his own
ground. But while he goes on, tranfgreffing the very
firft, and moft obvious, laws of all found reafoning,
fheltering himfelf under terms of doubtful fignifica-
tion, and ufing them in the moft loofe and ambiguous
manner, without ever deigning to drop a fingle hint, for
explanation; I fhall not fay " contempt," for I reckon
that unbecoming a Chriftian; but a "filent" bearing
of the abufe, will probably be the reply of Diffenters.
Pray, what fort of obedience is intended by Mr.
Fletcher? Is it paffive fubmiffion to thofe public burdens,
or general taxes, which are laid upon the fubjects, by
fuperior power; and levied, without afking any queftion,
for confcience' fake? Is it fimply doing thofe things,
which, for the matter of them, are good, and agreeable
to the moral law; whether the powers, in being, require them, or not? Or, is it a direct and proper recognizing of the authority; by openly approving. of the
conditions, on which it is held and exercifed; confenting to the lawfulnefs of the conftitution, by which only
it can be fupported; and folemnly profeffing or fwearing,
if required, to be faithful, and bear true allegiance to
the fovereign, as the power ordained of God, to whom
we muft be fubject for confcience' fake, and under pain
of condemnation? Let him tell us, what he underftands
by the obedience for which he pleads; and what it,
neceffarily, implies. We muft alfo have an explanation of the term, " Prefent civil Britifh Government."

Does

† Def. p. 100.

Does it mean the whole complex fyftem, in all its effential parts, taken as an united whole; and called,
The Britifh Conflitution? Or, are we to confider
Mr. Fletcher himfelf, though an avowed enemy to Magiftracy in the abftract, as abftracting the merely civil
parts of the conftitution, refpecting the life and property
of the fubject, from that very firft foundation-ftone, and
ground-work of the whole fabric, " That whofoever
fhall hereafter come to the poffeffion of this crown, fhall
join in communion with the church of England as by
law eftablifhed?" And, agreeable to this, he fhall be
confidered, " As the head and fupreme governor of the
national church;" viz. of England; " the DERNIER
RESORT in all ecclefiaftical caufes; an appeal lying ultimately to him in chancery from the fentence of every
ecclefiaftical judge." † Does Mr. Fletcher include,
or exclude thefe; when he fpeaks of the Britifh government? By the fundamental, and folemnly ratified laws
of the nation, they are infeparably connected with the
other effential, and component, parts of the conftitution.
Or, different from all thefe, are we to underftand him,
as meaning the perfons in power? But, if fo; whether
are they to be confidered fimply as men; or as men
clothed with official character, holding, and exercifing
magiftratical authority, folely on the footing of the
united Britifh Conftitution? Let our opponent explain himfelf; if he expect to be attended unto.

Perhaps forgetting that he had, no farther back than
the laft paragraph, thus cautioned his antagonift, " Let
not him that girdeth on his harnefs, boaft himfelf as he
that putteth it off;" Mr. Fletcher taketh unto himfelf
the buckler and fhield; and, having girded on his harnefs, with all the confequential airs of a Philiftian-
Champion, challenges his opponent, " Here, Sir, the
Loyalift once more defies you, or any other man, to
prove,—That it is the duty of Chriftians to difown
the authority of Chriftian Magiftrates, under whofe
government they enjoy their natural, civil, and religious

† BLACKSTONE.

T

ous privileges, and may lead a quiet and peaceable life, in all godlinefs and honefty." † Our friend, Mr. Fletcher, however, if he had thought it proper, might have faved himfelf the trouble of this bold defiance; till once he had fhewn us, in what part of their writings, Diffenters ever taught any fuch doctrine. So foon as he can tell, where they have afferted; they will, likely, be able to tell, how they can prove. So far are they from difowning fuch government; as properly anfwers to the above defcription, that earneftly contending for it, is one of their diftinguifhing characteriftics. Making violent encroachments on the royal prerogatives of Chrift, as fole King in Zion, and infringing the fpiritual liberties of his people, have ever been exhibited by them, as their greateft complaints, againft the conftitution of the government, Whether or not thefe complaints be juft, Mr. Fletcher, and the reader may fee, by confulting Mr. Steven's Pofthumous Letter, "Remark II. Concerning the Eraftianifm of the prefent times." As to living a quiet and peaceable life, in all godlinefs and honefty; the difciples of Jefus, as lambs in the midft of wolves, may, through the grace of God enabling them, conduct themfelves in a peaceful and inoffenfive manner, in as far as the matter refpects them, even under tyrants and ufurpers; and, much more, under rulers, comparatively mild and gentle; yet holding and exercifing their power, on conditions, deftructive of the religious liberty, wherewith Chrift hath made his people free.

† Def. p. 100.

ANI-

The attentive reader will eafily perceive, that this part of the Defence is moftly tranfcribed, in a very fervile manner, from the Loyalift. Proceeding in the form of inferences, from the doctrine taught in the body of the Book; we are not to expect proof, for the very grievous charges it contains; accordingly, we are troubled with none. One thing, very noticeable, is, that a fpirit of the moft bitter invective, though ftrongly blamed by Mr. Fletcher when found in others, breathes, with increafing vigour, in every fentence of this Conclufion. The pen, which was dipt in gall, at the writing of the Title-page, is kept in conftant employ, till the concluding fentence be finifhed. Here the Reformed Prefbytery are reprefented " as holding up fome of the plaineft precepts of the law of Chrift, to the derifion of infidels.—Their fenfelefs expofition of Rom. xiii. 1,—7. is," we are told, " a manifeft token, that they have departed from the faith once delivered to the faints, and are following cunningly-devifed fables.—The Reformed Brethren," it muft be feen, " are not going forth by the footfteps of Prophets, of Apoftles, and of Chrift." Even all this will not fuffice; it muft be added, " The beft apology, which a Reformed Prefbyterian can make for paying tribute, or for an involuntary way of finning, may be expreffed in the words of the Syrian general to the prophet Elifha: *When I bow down myfelf in the houfe of Rimmon, the Lord pardon thy fervant in this thing.*" † If the reader difcern, in thefe fayings, and there are many more of the fame kind, in the few pages of this Conclufion, that charity which thinketh no evil, a difpofition to render bleffing for railing, and the meek fpirit of thofe, who, when they are reviled, revile not again; his penetration, I muft confefs, is far beyond mine.

Whether

† Def. p. 101,—103.

T 2

Whether or not, our expofition of Rôm. xiii. 1.—7. be a fenfelefs expofition; and whether we pervert, and hold up to the derifion of infidels, or give the juft meaning of thefe plain precepts, to which, in the courfe of this dif-pute, our attention hath been called, muft now be fub-mitted to the decifion of the difcerning and impartial public ; as we are not, likely, for a time at leaft, to fay much more on fome of them, than what we have faid.

" The diftinction," fays Mr. Fletcher, " between a voluntary and involuntary way of paying tribute, is a moft enfnaring diftinction." * That, like many other neceffary, and important diftinctions, it is capable of being ftrained, and perverted, efpecially by fuch a writer as our opponent, will be readily granted. But is it not a juft diftinction ? Mr. Fletcher hath often fent us to the land of Egypt, to learn confcientious obedience unto lawful authority. Pray, was it voluntary, or in-voluntary obedience, which the fons of Jacob yielded, under the iron rod of their oppreffors, when they ferved with rigour, fulfilled their daily tafks, and, at the ex-pence of infupportable fatigue, gave in, as nearly as pof-fible, the full tale of the bricks, even when ftraw was denied them ? But I am, happily, prevented from de-taining the reader, on this topic, by the very full def-cription of it, in Mr. Steven's poithumous Letter. †
With refpect to Mr Fletcher's illiberal and ungenteel banter, concerning fuch things, as he fuppofes might be done, under the fanction of this diftinction; ‡ it pro-ceeds wholly upon the footing of manifeftly abufing the term, as a pretext for doing things, which are, in their own nature, pofitively finful, being direct viola-tions of the moral law ; and, therefore, can have no connection with the doctrine of Diffenters, on this head. When they, at any time, fpeak of involuntarily yielding to fome things, which are not objects of choice; they, uniformly, mean only fuch things, as are, in their nature, innocent, and do not neceffarily involve a breach of the divine law ; though, with refpect to the
prin-

* Def. p. 102. † p. 8,—13. ‡ Def. p. 102, 103.

principle from which, the manner, and the degree, in which they are required, it may be humbly apprehended by them, that the perfons in power act, without a pro-, per fcriptural warrant, and go beyond their commiffion.

It is expected, " the intelligent reader will fee, that the Reformed Brethren - are very juftly denominated, THE ANTIGOVERNMENT PEOPLE." † Since the com-, mencement of our diffent from the public deeds of the nation, we have openly, and uniformly, taught, that civil magiftracy is a precious ordinance, appointed by God, as the Great Creator of heaven and earth ; for promoting his own glory, and the happinefs of human fociety. We, every year, publicly, refufe to hold communion with fuch, as deny this divine inftitution, in New Teftament-times. We have, all along, contended for the Scriptural purity of civil government. We openly manifelt our earneft defire to fee it fettled on the fame ancient, and honourable footing; on which it ftood, in the days of our forefathers. And, even while we cannot obtain this, we endeavour to live peaceably with all men, giving no difturbance to our neighbours, but feeking the welfare of human fociety. If the reader be intelligent, and mean to fee, that fuch a people de-ferve the epithet of ANTIGOVERNMENT ; he would re-quire fome better evidence, than what is exhibited, in either the Loyalift, or the Defence. Becaufe the firft Seceders found, and declared, that the ecclefiaftical ju-dicatories, of that time, were not lawful, nor rightly conftituted courts of Chrift ; and fo declined their jurifdiction over them; ‡ did this fay, that the Seceders were ANTIGOVERNMENT-MEN, in refpect of ecclefiaftical authority ? Or, that they refufed obedience to the juft commands of lawful church-rulers ? I fuppofe, they would not thank us, for faying fo. No more con-fiftent can it ever be, to call us ANTIGOVERNMENT-MEN, in refpect of civil authority ; merely becaufe we find, and declare, that the prefent rulers hold, and exercife their power, on conditions, which appear unto us to be finful,

† Def. p. 103.

‡ See their Declinature, given in to the Affembly, May 17th. 1739.

finful, whether you fuppofe our opinion to be right, or wrong; and becaufe we declare, and affign our reafons for it, that the High Courts of Parliament are not rightly conftituted. Let Seceders, then, do unto others, as they would wifh others to do unto them; and we fhall never more be troubled with the malicious epithet, ANTIGOVERNMENT. †

It is next fuppofed, " That if the principles of the Reformed Brethren, about the civil government of Great Britain, were reduced to practice, all civil and natural relations among mankind, would be diffolved, and the whole world be a Babel of confufion.—The fervant may difown the authority of his mafter, and run away from his fervice; the fon may difown the authority of the father that begat him, and of the mother that brought him forth; and the wife may difown the authority of her hufband, may leave his bofom, and become another man's wife. Where is the mafter, the parent, or hufband, who doth not want this, and the other Scriptural qualification?" ‡ Strange reafoning, to be fure! Pray, what are our principles? Have they not, uniformly, been, That, according to the law of God, and the once fundamental laws of the kingdom, all places of power and truft, from the higheft to the loweft, in the nation, fhould be filled, on warrantable conditions of advancement; and by men, properly qualified, men profeffing the true Prefbyterian religion, fearing God, hating covetoufnefs, a terror to evil doers, and the praife of them that do well? What would the reducing of thefe principles to practice be? In the ordinary fenfe of language, at leaft, it would certainly be, Actually filling the feveral places of power and truft, in the manner now defcribed. Would this turn the whole world into a Babel of confufion? " No, indeed," it will be granted; " but when you cannot obtain this ftate of
things;

---

† On the inconfiftency of applying this epithet to Diffenters, fee the Letter, addreffed to the Burgher-Committee, by Mr. M'Millan of Stirling, p. 18, 19, 20.

‡ Def. p. 104.

things; you diffent, enter your public proteft, here is
the danger! and teftify againft filling the places of
power and truft, in any other manner; leaving the
majority of the nation, who have invefted the authorities, in their own way, alfo to fupport and defend them,
in their own way; while you, it cannot be refufed, ftill
live peaceably, and wifh to fubmit only to fuch things,
as are not inconfiftent with your public diffent, and
open profeffion." Be it fo. The firft Seceders found,
that the places of religious truft, in the church, were
not, at that time, filled in fuch manner, as they reckoned
indifpenfibly neceffary, both by the Word of God, and
Reformation-Acts of Affembly; they, therefore, protefted,
feceded, and refufed fubjection to the prevailing party,
in power; except upon fuch conditions, as the other
would never grant. Was this calculated to diffolve
all religious connections, and fubordination, in the
church? Did it warrant the diffatisfied individual, on
every whimfical pretence, to decline the authority of
his own Seffion; the Seffion to deny their fubordination
to the Prefbytery; the Prefbytery to difregard the deeds
of the Synod; and the Synod to counteract the decifions
of the General Affembly? The party, feceded from,
no doubt, both thought, and faid fo; but the feceding
party, I fuppofe, would not like the inference: no more
reafon have we, either to like or to admit it, in the
other cafe. That civil government, and ecclefiaftical
government, are fpecifically different, and that different
qualifications are requifite, for filling the refpective
places of truft, we readily acknowledge. At the fame
time, it cannot be denied, that the Word of God, and
Reformation-laws, prefcribe and enjoin, with equal
pointednefs and precifion, concerning the qualifications
of the one, and of the other. But even fuppofing it
were not fo; ftill the general principle is not affected:
if public diffent and teftimony, have a native tendency,
to diffolve civil relations, in the ftate; public diffent
and teftimony muft, upon the fame principle, have a
native tendency to diffolve religious connection, and

fubordi-

subordination, in the church. " Thou therefore which
teachelt another, teachest thou not thyself?"

However specious Mr. Fletcher's reasoning on this
head, may, at first glance, appear; the attentive reader
will soon discern its fallacy. In order to make the cases
parallel; one of two things, or both, must necessarily
be supposed: either, that these relations, mentioned,
are attempted to be forced upon a person, without any
proper reason for doing so; or else, that, being already
actually formed, something is done, altogether incon-
sistent with the nature of the relation, and subversive of
the very ends, for which it was formed. In such cases,
I should not be much astonished, to hear of disowning,
or dissolving. Were a servant to be forced to put himself under the authority of a master; upon conditions,
which he could by no means approve, and to which he
found it impossible for him, conscientiously, to consent,
suppose for less wages than he was willing to take, or
could live by; where would be the absurdity of refusing
such a man for his master? Or, if the relation were already formed, by mutual consent, but the master op-
pressed his servant, deprived him of his wages, and
openly violated the paction between them; who could
blame him, though, in such a case, he run away from
his service? In like manner; were a son forcibly required to own for his father, a person, who never begat
him, and with whom he wants to have no concern, and
to subject to the authority of a mother, who never
brought him forth; would it be any surprise, to find him
rejecting the proposal? Or say, they were his real pa-
rents; but have become cruel as the ostrich, deny him
his subsistence, beat, and abuse him; why should he
not be allowed to decline such jurisdiction? As to the
case of the wife; it is no less obvious, that no woman
could ever be expected to receive, for her husband, a
man, who is not the object of her choice; or to enter
into the conjugal relation, upon conditions, which she
could, by no means, approve. Supposing, on the other
hand, the relation to be voluntarily formed; but she,
afterwards, finds her husband, openly and habitually,

violat-

violating the marriage-covenant, and taking others into
his bofom ; would fhe be to blame for leaving it ? Two
of thefe three cafes, viz. that of the fervant and mafter,
and that of the wife and her hufband, may, if properly
attended to, ferve to illuftrate the fubject before us ;
as thefe relations, like that between magiftrate and
fubject, are formed by mutual confent, and proceed on
the footing of a paction between the parties. But the
other cafe, of parent and child, hath little, or no, refemblance ; feeing, in the forming of that relation, the
child is wholly paffive, and hath neither will, nor fay,
in the matter. Accordingly, unlefs he verily mean to
teach the doctrine of paffive-obedience, and to plead
the caufe of flavery ; Mr. Fletcher fhould no more
fpeak of the relation, between the parent and child, as
being parallel to that, between the prince and the people. With refpect to requifite qualifications ; to want
" this and the other qualification," is one thing : and
to want the very firft and principal qualifications, which
the Scriptures exprefsly require, and which the formerly
fundamental and folemnly ratified laws of the kingdom,
have made effential to the enjoying of regal dignity, is
another. The former will likely be the cafe, while we
are in this imperfect ftate ; for the latter, there is no
neceffity, but what arifes out of our grievous backfliding
from the righteous ways of God ; for which backfliding
it becomes neither Seceders nor Diffenters, to make
any apology.

I am aware, we fhall foon be told, that we have
compared the Britifh Rulers to the cruel and unrighteous mafter, and to the faithlefs hufband ; this, however,
is neither neceffarily implied, nor really intended. It
may indeed be the cafe, with refpect to fome things ;
and it may not be the cafe, with refpect to others. But
wherein we mean the parallel to hold, as to all rulers
in general, is chiefly this. As the above relations, cannot be properly formed, unlefs by mutual confent ; and
as, without that, the parties fhould not be forced upon
each other ; fo is it, in the cafe of the king, and his
fubjects : and, as thefe relations have their ftipulated
conditions, which muft be, mutually, agreed upon, as

the

the foundation of the obligation, to perform the refpective duties, which the parties owe to each other; fo fhould it be, with refpect to thefe rulers, whom we are required to own. Thofe, who deny this, will be found, in fpite of all defence, to plead the caufe of flavery: while thofe, who grant it, will eafily difcern, that Diffenting principles have not the remoteft tendency to diffolve either natural or civil relations amongft men. Nay, it is prefumed, that the refpective duties, of thefe feveral relations, were more faithfully, and confcentioufly performed; when all ranks, in this nation, generally, adopted, and folemnly fware to maintain, the very fame principles, for which Diffenters ftill contend; than what they are now, amidft all the new light, which mankind have got.

Would Mr. Fletcher allow himfelf, calmly and candidly, to confider the matter; it is prefumed, he could not but fee, that all focieties, in general, great and fmall, civil and ecclefiaftic, proceed upon the fame general principle, for which Diffenters contend. The qualifications for memberfhip, and conditions of advancement into office, may be rather of a different kind; they may be more, or fewer: but where is the corporation of any kind, which hath not fome prefcribed qualifications, not fimply declared to be ufeful, providing they can be found; but pofitively infifted upon, as fo indifpenfibly neceffary, that, without them, there is no admiffion into the fociety; nor any participation of its privileges and honours? If you maintain, that whatever fort of qualifications might be defirable, and exceedingly ufeful, if they could be obtained; yet none ought to be ftood upon, as effentially neceffary, for filling the places of public truft in a nation; then, with a witnefs, you lead the way, for turning the whole world into a Babel of confufion; you ftab the very vitals of every fociety upon earth. But if you grant, that, although not thofe for which we plead, yet fome qualifications fhould be infifted upon, as indifpenfibly neceffary; learn them from the law of nature, the law of Scripture, or from what other quarter you pleafe, let them be few, or let them be many; you go on the fame

gene-

general principle with ourfelves; and leave us room
to draw the fame inference, which you wifh to father
upon our doctrine. Suppofe you pofitively infift on
no other conditions than fimply protecting the natural
lives and civil liberties of the fubjects, and adminiftring
common juftice amongft them; inftances can be given,
in which even thefe have been totally awanting. But
if ftanding upon qualifications, which the exifting ruler
doth not actually poffefs, be introductive of anarchy
in one cafe, how is it not fo, in another, even granting
the refpective qualifications fhould be rather different,
in kind, or number: For illuftrating this, we need not
look farther than the monftrous Nero. Here is a prince,
who, inftead of protecting the natural lives of his fubjects, flaughtered them by hundreds, and made their
blood to run like water, merely to fatiate his own infernal cruelty. In place of defending their liberties;
he kept his beft fubjects, and oftentimes his neareft
friends, under a fyftem of conftant terror, till matters
arrived at fuch a pitch, that one companion durft
fcarcely be feen fpeaking with another, for fear of immediate impeachment. In the room of common juftice,
he plentifully adminiftred poifon, the halter, and the
confuming flames. † Would it have been unreafonable,
in this cafe, to have ftood on the few conditions laft
mentioned; and to have folemnly protefted, that Nero,
who thus hated right, fhould no longer reign? Or would
it have been more proper, to have argued thus: "However defirable it would be, to find our prince poffeffing
thofe qualifications; yet, feeing he actually has them
not, we muft take him as we find him; left we fhould
incur the guilt of holding principles, which, if reduced
to practice, would diffolve all relations among men,
and turn the whole world into a Babel of confufion?"
The ancient conditions of advancement to regal dignity,
in this nation, were, amongft other things, "That, before
the King's majefty who now is, or any of his fucceffors,
fhall be admitted to the exercife of his royal power,
he fhall affure and declare, by his folemn oath, under
his

† See the Annals of Tacitus.

his hand and feal, his allowance of the National Covenant, and of the Solemn League and Covenant, and
obligation to profecute the ends thereof, in his ftation
and calling. And fhall agree to Acts of Parliament
fully eftablifhing Prefbyterian Government, the Direc-
tory for Worfhip, Confeffion of Faith and Catechifms,
as they are approven by the General Affembly
of this Kirk, and Parliament of this kingdom, in all
his Majefty's dominions; and that he fhall obferve
thefe in his own practice and family; and that he fhall
never make oppofition to any of thefe, or endeavour
any change thereof." † The conditions of advancement now are, amongft other things. " That the prince
be of the Hanoverian line, being Proteftant; that he
join in Communion with the church of England as by
law eftablifhed; and that he fupport and maintain
Prelacy inviolable, in England and Ireland." How
comes it, that the former conditions, pofitively infifted
upon, in the time of Reformation, and ftill. contended
for by Diffenters, lead to the diffolution of all relations
amongft mankind; while the later, no lefs pofitively
infifted upon now, are fully confiftent with " preferving
the honour, and performing the duties, belonging to
every one in their feveral places and relations?" Is it
merely, becaufe the former are fuppofed to be done
away; whereas the later really exift, by the will of
thofe, who act as reprefentatives of the nation? Still
the queftion recurs : How came they into exiftence;
without teaching fuch doctrine, " as tends to turn the
whole world into a Babel of confufion?" Had it not
been, that the above feems ftill to be confidered, as the
greateft, and moft formidable objection, on which both
Burghers, and Antiburghers, chiefly infift, in all their
writings, and difcourfes, againft Diffenters; I fhould not
have faid fo much upon it here.

In oppofition to what he finds, in Mr. Thorburn's
Book, our opponent goes on, to declare, " It is a downright falfehood, That the true religion is for ever excluded from the Britifh Conftitution." ‡ The farther
we

† Parl. 1649. Seff. 2. Act 15.   ‡ Def. p. 104;—105.

we proceed in this difpute; the more reafon we fee, for always being careful to define our terms. How forbidding does it look, to find two parties of profeffing Prefbyterians, both wifhing to contend for the faith once delivered to the faints, or two refpectable gofpel-minifters, giving the lie, the one to the other! This would have been prevented, at once, in the cafe before us, by explaining the term TRUE RELIGION. When Diffenters, in managing this controverfy, fpeak of the true religion; they mean, as their worthy anceftors did before, The true Proteftant, Prefbyterian, and covenanted religion, as it is to be found delineated in the Word of God, fummarily comprehended in our fubordinate Standards, and folemnly fworn to, in our National Vows to the Moft High God. That this true religion, formally confidered, is, for ever excluded from the Britifh Conftitution, by the publicly ratified Articles of the Union, and other fundamental laws of the kingdom, is a ftubborn, and incontrovertible fact. But Mr. Fletcher, by the true religion, muft underftand the Proteftant religion, taken in a loofe and vague fenfe, and comprehending alike both Prelacy and Prefbytery, as oppofed to Popery. Unlefs he have " unhappily got into the ftrong-hold of religion in the abftract;" and not as it is openly profeffed and practifed, in the land. There have been Seceders, who themfelves allowed, " That under the prefent Conftitution, a mighty bar is thruft into the way of our Covenanted Reformation, both in Church and State; yea, a grave ftone is laid and eftablifhed upon the fame." And, " That the Body-Politic have never, by their deed of civil conftitution, provided that their Magiftrates be brought under, and admitted upon obligations and terms, fuch as were fixed upon and eftablifhed in reforming periods, but fuch as are, in many refpects, not only different from, but deftructive of the fame, unto the great prejudice of REAL RELIGION, and reformation in the houfe of God." † Even this is fomewhat like an exclufion of
that,

---

† Decl. & Def. of Princ. p. 51.

that, which both they and we feem to have underftood by the true, or real, religion. But, fays Mr. Fletcher, " The King is obliged by oath, to maintain, to the ut- moft of his power, the laws of God, the true profeffion of the gofpel, and the Proteftant religion." † Why has he not added the remaining words of the very fame fentence, as it ftands in the coronation-oath, *viz.* " eftab- lifhed by the law?" No doubt, the attentive reader would then have feen, at once, that Prelacy, in England and Ireland, and a fort of Prefbytery in Scotland, were intended by the Proteftant religion, which the King fwears to maintain; and, confequently, that the cove- nanted uniformity, folemnly fworn unto, in the time of Reformation, was for ever excluded and deftroyed. Had Mr. Fletcher alfo condefcended to exhibit before his reader the next queftion and anfwer, in the corona- tion-oath; it would have made the matter quite plain. " Will you preferve unto the bifhops and clergy of this realm, and to the churches committed to their charge, all fuch rights and privileges as by law do or fhall ap- pertain unto them, or any of them?—King or Queen. All this I promife to do." But we muft alfo be told, by our opponent, " It is no lefs falfe, that the profeffion, prefervation and maintenance of idolatry, are the ef- fential conditions of holding the fupreme, or any civil power in thefe nations." As Diffenters have fufficiently explained themfelves, on this head; Mr. Fletcher cannot but know, that by idolatry here they underftand the will-worfhip and fuperftitious ceremonies of the church of England. That the maintenance of thefe is one effential condition of holding the fupreme power, he will not, furely, deny. Times have been, when Seceders them- felves did not think very favourably of this condition. " At the Union 1707," fay they, " a further, and very lamentable ftep of defeétion was made, in our civil fettlement; in regard the maintenance and prefervation of the Hierarchy and ceremonies of the church of Eng- land, is a fundamental and effential article of the faid

Union

† Def. p. 105.

Union." * If either our opponent, or the reader, fuppofe idolatry to be a falfe charge, upon the church of
England; it might not be amifs to recommend unto
their ferious perufal a fermon entitled, " Prelacy an Idol,
and Prelates Idolaters: All Prelatifts, Maintainers of,
and Compliers with Prelacy, charged with Idolatry,
and proven guilty." †

" The Loyalift," we are next informed, " has no ill-
will at the people called Old Diffenters." It may be fo.
Perhaps his pen has been guided by fome fudden guft of
paffion, rather than by his prevailing difpofition. It is
not our province, neither fhall we prefume, to tell, what
are the real fentiments of his heart. But had we proceeded by the general rule, That out of the abundance
of the heart, the mouth fpeaketh; we fhould, certainly,
have been led to a conclufion, rather unfavourable:
Such ftriking appearances of fpite, refentment, and deep-
rooted prejudice, as thofe with which the Defence is
fraught, will feldom, I apprehend, be found, in fo fmall
a compafs. Even the Loyalift himfelf, furrly as he
looks, is mild, when compared with his Defender. As
to " difloyalty, and turning rebels to government, from
a pretence of piety, fuppofed to be the moft effectual
fcheme, which even the Devil himfelf could recommend,
for blafting the honour of religion;" ‡ I hope, Diffenters
fhall be directed and enabled, freely to forgive Mr.
Fletcher, for laying any fuch thing to their charge.

We are very folemnly cautioned, to beware of " re-
viving the ancient and hellifh calumny againft the city
of our God, That—it is a rebellious city, and hurtful
unto kings and provinces." ‖ A good advice can never
be unfeafonable, if it have a proper object; but, pray,
what doth our friend's arguing reprove? If he mean,
that we fhould not give any real ground, for rational, and unprejudifed men, to bring a charge, of this
kind, againft the church and people of God; we heartily
concur with him; and are not confcious of being any
more

---

* Decl. & Def. of Prin. p. 50,—51.   † By Mr. Frafer of Brae.
‡ See Def. p. 105,   ‖ p. 106.

more blameable than our neighbours, on this fcore. But if he mean, that we fhould neither do, nor fay any thing; which may be, readily, mifreprefented, and fhamefully perverted, by the malevolent enemies of the church, fuch as were the calumniators, who anciently raifed this cry; it is much the fame as to fay, that we fhould not be valiant for the truth upon the earth: for it is certain, that the teftimony of Jefus hath always been tormenting, unto the carnal world. The truth ever hath found, and to the end of time, likely, will find malicious oppofers; ready to fay of even the moft harmlefs difciples, "Thefe, who have turned the world upfide-down, are come hither alfo." Notwithftanding the generous, the mild, and gentle conduct of the meek and lowly Jefus; even HE was condemned by his accufers, as a perverter of the nation, and an enemy to Cefar. The difciple need not expect to be above his Lord.

Before he part, the Loyalift, it feems, muft in his own way, teftify his friendfhip for his opponents. "The Reformed Prefbytery, and their followers," fays he, "will not think it a compliment, neverthelefs the Loyalift cordially wifhes, that the fire of their mifplaced, though well-meant zeal, about civil government, may be extinguifhed; and that the vail of ignorance and prejudice may be removed from their minds."—† In this, I prefume, Mr. Fletcher hath rightly judged. Diffenters have certainly much more reafon to confider his parting with as an infult, than as any compliment. Its meaning may, perhaps, be good; but it has a very furrly countenance. In thefe days of Jacob's trouble, Diffenters, as well as others, have more need to improve, than to extinguifh their zeal, for the declarative glory of God, and the beft interefts of human fociety. What they may be left to do, in the hour of temptation, it is not their's to fay; they have much to fear, but nothing to boaft. In dependance, however, on the God of their fathers,

† Def. p. 106, 107.

fathers, they wifh to live and die, endeavouring to contend for the faith once delivered unto the faints.

After a declaration, that if the Lord fhall be pleafed to blefs the Defence, for preventing oppofition to the truth, the labour will not be in vain; Mr. Fletcher concludes with a, feemingly, folemn wifh, that Mr. Steven " may never more be employed in publifhing falfehoods, contradictions, mifreprefentations, and malignant infinuations;—that he may no more pervert and abufe the Scriptures of truth for defending a caufe which is altogether indefenfible; and that his tongue may be, not as a fpear and arrow, to flay the reputation of his neighbour; but as choice filver, to fpeak forth the words of truth and fobernefs." † The pen, dipt in the bitter gall, muft ftill be employed, to bid his opponent adieu. The concluding words, indeed, are fmooth; but they are clofely attended by very haggard and forbidding companions.

After carefully perufing his Letter, and ferioufly reflecting on what, as it is well known, he uniformly delivered, in his difcourfes from the pulpit, the candid and unbiaffed public fhall be freely left to determine, whether or not Mr. Steven ever publifhed any fuch things, as are here afcribed unto him. Hundreds, whofe teftimony will be reckoned as valid as either Mr. Fletcher's or mine, can atteft, that he never, while in life, proftituted either his tongue, or his pen, to publifh fo much as one of thofe things, which are contained in this very grievous, and totally unfounded charge. Now, that he hath finifhed his courfe, fought the good fight, and, as we may charitably fuppofe, laid hold on eternal life; none can be any more in danger from him. Meanwhile, if Mr. Fletcher, or any other for him, will venture to fpecify one fingle falfehood, that ever was publifhed by our deceafed friend; fome Diffenter, or other, it is hoped, will be found to fhew becoming refpect unto the memory of the dead; who can no more take unto himfelf the buckler and fhield.

X

† Def. p. 107.

But I am now heart-fick of following our Author, fo long, and through fuch a very dreary rod. I feel difpofed to drop my pen for ever, in this controverfy; if it is any more to be managed, in the manner of the Defence. Were queftions to be fairly ftated, terms carefully explained, and the argument conducted with a chriftian fpirit; light might be thrown upon the fubject, and information received even from the difagreeable employment of taking different fides. But if thefe are not to be attended unto; I fhould reckon it much better to drop the difpute altogether; and fpend our leifure-hours, if leifure-hours we have, in fome more profitable exercife. Minifters are certainly fet for the defence of the gofpel, and of all the precious doctrines, contained in the Scriptures at large, whatever divine inftitution they refpect. Called, by their adored Mafter, to promote the beft interefts of his kingdom; they fhould never unfaithfully conceal the words of the Holy One, upon any fubject; but be valiant for the truth, in all its branches. Notwithftanding, if we are not allowed to have any precife fubject, or diftinct queftion, on which we are to give our opinion; but muft follow our oppofers, through a ·multiplicity of doctrines, which we never once called in queftion, and concerning which we hold no opinions peculiar to ourfelves; why fhould we thus labour for nought, and fpend our ftrength in vain?

Having endeavoured to ftate the queftion, and diveft the difpute of many things, which appear quite foreign to the fubject; if any reply is to be made; I hope, I fhall be allowed to infift, that the arguments, fuch as they are, which have been advanced, in thefe Animadverfions, fhall be fairly met. If it be thought, that they are not to the purpofe; let this be proved, and illuftrated. If they are found weak; the tafk of overturning them, will be the eafier. If any of them fhould happen to be ftrong; it would be more honeft, to acknowledge it, than to pafs them with a fneer.——Let it, therefore, be underftood, that unlefs we are to

meet

meet in fair combat; I fhall reckon myfelf, from henceforth, excufed, in paying no attention, to what may be advanced, on the other fide.

It is, in our times, a mournful truth, that there are many real differences of opinion, amongft the profeffing difciples of Jefus. Very few, I believe, will be found, in any fociety, who cordially agree, in the fame fentiment, concerning either the doctrine, worfhip, difcipline, or government of the New Teftament church; though thefe are, furely, very plainly taught us, in the facred Oracles. With refpect to the nature, and proper tendency of the feveral Reformation-attainments, in the laft century, the diverfity of opinion is no lefs ftriking. At the fame time, it is fufficiently obvious, that the differences are often multiplied, and exceedingly aggravated, by mifunderftanding, or mifreprefenting each other. Againft this, therefore, we fhould all be careful to guard. It brings much difhonour upon the common caufe of Chriftianity; gives great occafion unto our adverfaries, to load even the gofpel of peace, with reproach; and confirms the avowed infidel, in his falfe opinion, that even the moft zealous profeffors of religion believe not in its reality, any more than he. It is humbly apprehended, that, through the divine bleffing, it might alfo be of no fmall advantage, amidft our rending divifions, were we all, ferioufly, to concur, in confidering, and lamenting over them, as an awful token of the Lord's righteous difpleafure; a melancholy proof, that he hath, in a very fenfible manner, " forfaken his houfe, left his heritage; and given the dearly beloved of his foul into the hand of her enemies." Surely it is for a lamentation, on gofpel-Lebanon, " that the Great Shepherd, provoked by our fins, hath cut afunder his ftaff, even bands, that he may break the brotherhood between Judah and Ifrael." Reflecting on this, we have much reafon to fay, with the weeping Prophet, " How hath the Lord covered the daughter of Zion with a cloud in his anger, and caft down from heaven unto the earth the

the beauty of Ifrael, and remembred not his footftool in the day of his anger!"

May the God of Peace, who alone can do it, Turn to his people a pure language, that they may all call upon the name of the Lord, to ferve him with one confent; difpofe the profeffors of religion, to love the peace and the truth, in clofe connection; and haften the glory of the latter day, when the multitude of thofe who believe fhall, again, be of one heart, and one foul.

T H E   E N D.

www.ingramcontent.com/pod-product-compliance
Lightning Source LLC
Chambersburg PA
CBHW020555270326
41927CB00006B/848